Love God,
Change the World

**Inspiring today's college students
and
young professionals to make a difference**

Troy A. Criss

Love God, Change the World

© 2012 by Troy A. Criss and Illumination Publishers

Printed in the United States of America.

ISBN: 978-0-9855749-0-1

Unless otherwise indicated, all Scripture references are from the Holy Bible, New International Version, copyright 1973, 1978, 1984, 2011 by the International Bible Society. Used by permission of Zondervan Bible Publishers. All rights reserved.

Interior book design: Toney C. Mulhollan. The text face is typeset in Chaparral Pro and Helvetica. Cover design: Mykl Gormley.

Any Internet addresses printed in this book are offered as a resource. They are not intended in any way to be or imply an endorsement by Illumination Publishers.

Illumination Publishers is committed to caring wisely for God's creation and uses recycled paper whenever possible.

We pray that you benefit from this book by Illumination Publishers. Our goal is to provide high-quality, biblically based books and products that lead you to a deeper and more committed walk with God. For more information on books and audio/video teaching sets, go to www.ipibooks.com.

A special thanks to Amy Morgan for her editorial work.

www.ipibooks.com

Illumination Publishers International
www.ipibooks.com
6010 Pinecreek Ridge Court
Spring, Texas 77379-2513, USA

*To my high school sweetheart
and beautiful wife, Kim.
Your love for God and for other people
constantly pushes me outside
of my comfort zone.
Thank you for that.
You are truly my best friend.*

—Troy

Special thanks to...

Jeff Chacon for all your editing and encouragement.
This book would not have happened without your help.

Randy Scott, Sherwin Mackintosh, and Alan Henry
for being the best elders a man could ask for.

Kyle Eastman for serving the church and the
campus ministry that God has given us to lead.

The members of the Gainesville Christian Church
for seeking after the Lord with me.
Let's love God and change the world together.

In Christ,
Troy

Table of Contents

Foreword

Troy Criss's message is as simple as it is clear: Let's love God and change the world!

God is leading and empowering a new generation to change themselves so that they can change the world. "I firmly believe that the high school students, the college students and the young professionals hold the key to changing the course of the world. Are you up for it? Are you willing to do your part as an individual? Are you willing to work with a group of Christians to do your part collectively?" Troy offers this conviction and asks these questions with penetrating clarity.

I agree wholeheartedly with this perspective. We both share this conviction and hope for this generation. I value this book even more because I also respect greatly the author for his life, ministry, family and influence.

I remember meeting Troy and his dynamic wife, Kim, on a trip to Gainesville in 2005. Since I was baptized through the influence of the campus ministry at the University of Florida as a freshman in 1969, I have always had a special place in my heart for Gainesville. I was truly inspired to see all the young people in Troy's campus and professional ministries who were fired up for God!

Not only has Troy been leading the Gainesville Christian Church since 1999, he has had a large impact on campus ministries around the United States. Because of his example of building campus ministries, Troy was asked in 2006 to serve on an international campus committee called the Campus Service Team. The focus of this committee is to promote campus excellence around the world, mobilize college students for maximum impact, and organize International Campus Ministry Conferences (ICMC). Every summer for the past 6 years, Troy has helped to organize and promote these ICMCs in Los Angeles, Boston, Baton Rouge, Virginia Beach, Chicago, and Athens. The attendance has grown from about 1000 to almost 2500. These conferences serve to inspire college students to grow higher and dig deeper with the Lord while also giving students an opportunity to serve the poor. In 2008, for example, Troy helped organize 1800 college students to serve in the Lower Ninth Ward of New Orleans, Louisiana after it had been devastated by Hurricane Katrina. Of all the cleanup efforts that have occurred in New

Orleans since the hurricane, this was the largest single cleanup effort by any one group. It was truly a great day.

In the early 2000s many leaders from around the country encouraged our high school graduates to consider attending the University of Florida, primarily because of the powerful campus ministry in Gainesville. In Southern California where my wife, Kelly, and I were ministering at the time, we sent many of our young people to be influenced and inspired at the Gainesville Christian Church under Troy's leadership.

Troy Criss writes like he lives: straightforward, direct, full speed ahead and with conviction. He has always been devoted to excellence and organization. Nothing seems to slip through the cracks in his ministry as people are taken care of as well as taught. His commitment to his family has never allowed his ministry responsibilities to overshadow the priority of their needs. Those who know him best see him as serious but laid back. His very successful ministry is also a very healthy place to live and grow in Christ.

Troy is described as a fabulous preacher. His probing questions hit every segment of his listeners. However, raising up leaders is his passion and focus. He has been a catalyst in campus ministry for many years, as well as an advocate of teens, college students and young professionals taking their place to lead in the kingdom of God. Troy has also become a personal friend of mine as well as a valued partner in the ongoing quest to equip, inspire and train the next generation.

The strength of this book is not just in its considerable inspiration, but its practical instruction and direction. Troy mentors the reader to follow in the steps of the greatest game changer and world transformer the world has ever known...he enrolls us in the school of Dr. Jesus. He helps us practically in our commitment to be a genuine disciple ("learner") and a genuine follower, not just a believer who is tagging along.

In this book, the principles of loving God are combined with a radical call to action. An example is the chapter on "Pray Like Your Life Depends On It." A believer's prayer life can be so shallow, too often self-reliant. Troy tells us it is time for crazy prayers. He challenges his readers: "...often as Christians, our prayers are safe. We pray for good health, safe travels on a particular journey, protection for our family or children, rescue from financial problems,.... One thing that really gets God excited is to see his children praying crazy, radical prayers."

This book is unique in its extensive treatment and specific direction on how to organize and structure a disciple's life for maximum impact. An example of its immensely practical nature is the instruction on how to use a prayer sheet to help you stay organized in your prayer life. The prayer sheet organizer found in that chapter will help many. The book often reads like a field manual on radical living.

In his chapter on practicals on how one person can change the world, here is some of his direction:

-How can I change the world? One person at a time.
-How can I change the world? Live cheap and donate.
-How can I change the world? Mentor a child.
-How can I change the world? Be salty.

Troy does not hesitate to prod us to be like Jesus and the prophets of the Bible as we confront our culture. We need to do more than just avoid the darkness; rather, we must expose it (Ephesians 5:11). On our campuses and in our community, are we ready to challenge the status quo on its attitudes toward sexual purity, prejudice, the role and priority of the family, etc.?

This book asks us the question: How can the Christians change the world? And Troy provides an answer: Sometimes, we just need crazy faith! Crazy love for Christ produces crazy faith in the life of a disciple. Our need is to truly believe that we can do incredible things through God and his Spirit even if it seems impossible to others. Everyone agrees that the problems in the world are simply too enormous and systemic to change by religion or even devotion. However, when Christians are united together with crazy faith and motivated by crazy love, that is a combination that cannot be defeated.

The sincere and humble reader will also appreciate that Troy Criss does not pull any punches or over qualify. His chapter "Living on the Wrong Side of Easter" once again shoots straight: "Most people are not willing to give up everything for Jesus. They value their 'things,' their time or their lives too much to give up everything for God's kingdom. They are content with being lukewarm and even warn others not to 'go overboard with religion.' What they do not realize is that giving up everything is a requirement for passage into God's eternal home."

This is a clarion and uncompromising call. It penetrates as it addresses our often superficial and inherited version of Christianity. Does this remind you of somebody? "In the same way, any of you who does not give up everything he has cannot be my disciple" (Luke 14:33). I love the repeated calls to action, to not just love God, but to change the world (John 14:15, 20:21; Matthew 28:18–20). Jesus' call was radical: DROP EVERYTHING YOU ARE DOING and come together to change the world! It did not matter to Jesus who you were or what you were doing.

You will enjoy and be inspired by the actual accounts of real people who made radical decisions. You will be challenged, inspired to change and inspired to call others to do the same. This is not just for the young, but also for men and women of all ages whose desire is to love God with all of their heart, mind and strength, and whose heart is still to change the world, not just survive it. This is a call for many of us to be reawakened, refocused and renewed in a decision we made years ago.

This is especially true for those who have taken up the biblical pattern and challenge for the older to teach the younger: to mentor, to disciple, to train, to lead and to impact. For those who have been paying attention, there is also a growing army of experienced disciples of Christ who are not settling for comfort or spiritual retirement. They are refusing to relegate themselves to being backseat drivers in God's kingdom instead of their godly appointed role as sages, trainers and examples in a continuing quest to win the world. Those readers will find their hearts stirred.

Twelve years ago, the campus ministry and the impact young people were making on the church had waned. Over the last twelve years Troy Criss has been a herald, sometimes a voice in the wilderness, of restoring vision and evangelistic impact in campus ministry. He is a church planter and a trainer. No single minister or evangelist I have known in recent years has trained more full-time ministry workers as well as equipped hundreds who have taken their places in churches around the world. These are well-balanced young men and women who have excelled in academics, athletics, their careers and most importantly, their impact on God's church.

In conclusion, read these pages—learn the secrets, master the principles and embrace the practicals this book offers you. "It is time to rouse the warriors! There is much to do and we cannot do it alone." As Jesus said in Mark 10:27, "With man this is impossible, but not with God; all things are possible with God."

—Tom Brown,
North River Church of Christ, Atlanta, Georgia

Part One

Love God

Chapter One

Do You Hear the Alarm?

Mary: "I'd say your chances are more like one out of a million."
Harry: "So...you're telling me there's a chance! YEAH!"

—*Dumb and Dumber*

Sometimes we just don't get it. We think that we are listening to what someone is saying but really we are not hearing them at all. We are simply hearing what we want to hear, what we hope they are saying to us.

I believe that God is sounding an alarm right now and most of us do not hear it. How can we? Most of us are so distracted by our fast-paced schedules and personal ambitions that we fail to hear the crying of the Holy Spirit. Please slow down for a moment and consider these facts:

Divorce Rate in the US
- 45–50% of all first marriages in the U.S. end in divorce.
- 60–67% of all second marriages in the U.S. end in divorce.
- 70–73% of all third marriages in the U.S. end in divorce.[1]

Children Born Out of Wedlock

- In 2007, nearly 40% of all U.S. births were to unmarried women. In 1980, that rate was only 18.4%.[2]
- Current trends indicate that by the year 2015, 50% of all American babies will be born to a single mother. At that time, illegitimacy will surpass divorce as the main cause of fatherlessness.[3]
- Nearly half of pregnancies among American women are unintended; about four in ten of these pregnancies are terminated by abortion.
- 22% of all U.S. pregnancies end in abortion (Alan Guttmacher Institute).
- In 2007, 84% of all abortions were performed on unmarried women (Centers for Disease Control and Prevention).
- 50% of U.S. abortions are by women younger than twenty-five years old.[4]

Pornography

- Eleven is the average age when a person first views pornography.
- The word "porn" is the #4-ranked searched term by kids under seven years old.
- Nearly half of all divorces list pornography as a contributing factor.[5]
- In 2006, the worldwide pornographic industry had revenue of over $97 billion (that is more than Microsoft, Google, Amazon, eBay, Yahoo, Apple, and Netflix...combined!)
- Forty million adults visit pornographic websites daily.
- 28,258 Internet users are viewing pornography...*every second*.[6]

Teenage Suicide
- Each year in the US, thousands of teenagers commit suicide. Suicide is the third leading cause of death for fifteen- to twenty-four-year-olds, and the sixth leading cause of death for five- to fourteen-year-olds.[7]

Drug Use
- The average age of first marijuana use in the U.S. is fourteen.

Right now you might be thinking, "But how can I really help? I'm just one person. What does God really expect *me* to do?" For starters, simply recognize the alarm.

In the book of Joel, God begins to sound the alarm for his people living in Judah and Jerusalem. God was looking at the all of the devastation going on in the land and was not calling for the outsiders to repent but rather for **his people to repent!** Please allow me to give you a sampling:

> Hear this, you elders;
>> listen, all who live in the land.
> Has anything like this ever happened in your days
>> or in the days of your forefathers? (1:2)

> A nation has invaded my land,
>> powerful and without number;
> it has the teeth of a lion,
>> the fangs of a lioness. (1:6)

> Put on sackcloth, O priests, and mourn;
>> wail, you who minister before the altar. (1:13a)

Declare a holy fast;
　　call a sacred assembly. (1:14a)

Blow the trumpet in Zion;
　　sound the alarm on my holy hill. (2:1)

"Even now," declares the LORD,
　　"return to me with all your heart." (2:12a)

Return to the LORD your God,
　　for he is gracious and compassionate. (2:13)

Gather the people,
　　consecrate the assembly;
bring together the elders,
　　gather the children,
　　those nursing at the breast.
Let the bridegroom leave his room
　　and the bride her chamber. (2:16)

Proclaim this among the nations:
　　Prepare for war!
Rouse the warriors! (3:9a)

Do you notice the severity of the alarm? Everybody was expected to respond to it, including the infants who were being nursed by their mothers. You were expected to respond even if it was your wedding today and you were just moments from the ceremony! Wow! The call was radical: **DROP EVERYTHING YOU ARE DOING AND COME TOGETHER TO CHANGE THE WORLD!**

It did not matter who you were or what you were doing. This was a call for all of God's people to come together, hear the alarm, notice the devastation, and repent of *their sins*. They had become a nation of self-indulgent people who had begun to value material things over spiritual things. God was not willing to change the devastation until his people were ready to change.

Do you hear the alarm going off? Do you see the devastation occurring in our world today? Do you hear God calling you and me to make a difference?

In order to change this world, we must first convince young people of one simple truth: It's not about you. Your life is not about your life. At least, it is not supposed to be. God did not design for us to live that way, but the world definitely trains us to think that way. We would never say that "life is all about me," but often we think it and, more importantly, we live it. Have you ever looked at a large group photograph that you were in? Of all the people, who did your eyes go to first? If you are anything like me, you looked at yourself first. You looked to see if your eyes were closed or if your smile was just right. You checked out your appearance first before noticing anyone else. We may not consciously do it, but it is our nature to put our own needs above the needs of others. It is our tendency to love ourselves first. As Paul says "Do nothing out of selfish ambition or vain conceit, but in humility consider others better than yourselves" (Philippians 2:3). I believe this is also why Jesus said the second greatest commandment is to "love your neighbor as yourself" (Matthew 22:39). The implication is that we already know how to love ourselves really well.

This world is about God and God alone. After all that God has done to create the universe, mankind, animals and the ecosystem in which we survive, it is crazy for us to think that this world is about us. But we are tempted to believe so. Do you realize that approximately 100 billion people have walked this earth, lived their relatively short lives, and subsequently died before you were ever born? Think about that: About 100,000,000,000 people lived on earth before you—that's a lot! Here's a crazy thought: Outside of perhaps a few hundred of them, you do not know any of their names or what their lives were about. Do you realize that about 50 to 100 years after your death, there will most likely not be a single person on the planet who knows that you ever existed? Think about it: Outside of famous performers, politicians, philanthropists, and discoverers, who from the past can you name beyond your grandparents? Anyone? Seriously, try it. So unless you discover the cure for a disease or get some football stadium named after you, your name will likely disappear someday. That is a sobering thought, isn't it? If we know that our name will disappear someday, why do we work so hard to gain recognition? That's like working for many hours to create a beautiful drawing on the beach sand, knowing that high tide will arrive soon to wash it all away. Nobody would do that, and yet I watch so many people working feverishly to build their own lives, not realizing that they are building in vain. Instead of focusing so much on our own lives, we ought to slow down enough to realize who this world's story is really about: God.

In 1994, I graduated from the University of North Florida with a bachelor's degree in mathematics. After graduation, I got married to my high school sweetheart and joined the U.S. Navy to learn how to operate nuclear reactors on submarines. Before I began to do all the cool things that I envisioned doing in the military, do you know what was the first thing I did when I arrived at boot camp? As soon as I stepped off the bus on day one in Great Lakes, Chicago, the chief directed all of the recruits (not very politely, I might add) to go into this large gymnasium, take off all of our clothes, put them into a box, label it with a mailing address, and ship it all back home. My designer jeans, favorite T-shirt, jacket, brand new tennis shoes, gold necklace I had been wearing since sixth grade, cool watch, baseball hat, wedding ring...everything that defined me (or at least, so I thought) was just stripped from me in the first fifteen minutes of my arrival at boot camp. In their place, I was given a one-size-fits-all Navy blue sweat suit. Even though I was wearing clothes, I felt naked and alone. Immediately after they collected all of our boxes for shipping, they lined us up to get hair cuts. This was no ordinary barber. You did not get to request how you wanted your hair to be cut. There was no "just take a little off the sides." Nope. There were five barber chairs in a room and you just waited until a barber yelled, "Next!" The haircut only took about twenty seconds to perform—shaved everything off. All you could see was my white scalp. I had been at boot camp for about one hour at this point and I no longer recognized myself. Why did the Navy do this to me? I believe the Navy had one message and I heard them loud and clear: "It's not about you. You may have arrived here thinking you have your own style, your own flavor, and you deserve special treatment. Not anymore. This is not about you. Rather, it's about the group. It's about our common mission. It's about what we can accomplish together if we put our differences aside and focus on our purpose."

In John 12:24, Jesus said, "I tell you the truth, unless a kernel of wheat falls to the ground and dies, it remains only a single seed. But if it dies, it produces many seeds." Jesus said this on Palm Sunday, right after his triumphal entry into Jerusalem. Thousands of people had just praised him publicly and placed palm branches on the ground before him (used in celebration of victory; see Revelation 7:9–17). Yet Jesus knew that in five days he would horrifically die on a cross and all these people would desert him! His point in John 12:24 was that if you really want to follow him, if you really want your life to produce something great for God, it is going to take more than lip service. It is going to require personal sacrifice. It is going to require that you let go of everything worldly that you think makes you who you are and allow God to rebuild you in his image.

Before you ask the question, "How can I help?"—I want to first make sure that you hear the alarm. Do you hear it yet? I believe that God wants to rouse the warriors in his kingdom and use his followers to change the world! I believe the call of the hour is not for the world to repent, but rather for the disciples of Jesus to repent. This world is a mess, and God is calling us to repent of our selfishness so that we can finish the work of Jesus Christ. In order to change our planet's current path of unspirituality, we must be willing to be that kernel of wheat that falls to the ground and dies for the greater cause. Brothers and sisters, we must live today like we will die tomorrow. Better yet, we must die today like we will live tomorrow.

Small Group Discussion Questions for Chapter One

1. Which of the statistics in this chapter stood out to you or affected you the most? Why?

2. Why do so many people work feverishly to build their own lives here on earth? Do you tend to focus more on your short, earthly life or your long, eternal life? What does a person's life look like who is focused on eternity?

3. Do you believe that God is sounding an alarm? Do you believe that God's people have a responsibility to help change the world?

Chapter Two

Passing the Spiritual Exam

Tom Cruise: "I want the truth!"
Jack Nicholson: "You can't handle the truth!"

—*A Few Good Men*

One thing I love about young people: They want to hear the truth! They want the word of God preached hot! They don't want a small portion of a soft sermon delivered by an overweight preacher. They do not respect that. No, they want to hear the word of God preached with passion and conviction from someone who is displaying it in his own life. That is what college students and young professionals crave. (Whether or not they accept the message and apply it to their lives is another question entirely.)

Young people crave a radical purpose. If they do not find it in Jesus, they will look for it in other areas like academia, student government, dating, video games, gambling, sports, writing or playing music, making money or even partying. Every time I study the Bible with a college student who is seeking a relationship with God, it only takes a few minutes to discover what his or her current purpose is. It's easy: Just listen to them talk. What you talk about most is usually your biggest focus in life. I have studied with students who play *HALO* or *Worlds of Warcraft* for two to ten hours per day and plan their day around their time in front of the computer. They are addicted to it. I have studied with students who have been in a serious dating relationship for years, are sexually active with their partner, and communicate through phone calls and texting about thirty to forty times throughout the day. They are addicted to each other. I have studied with college students who are excessive in their study of schoolwork. They can only see as far as their next exam and will back out of all previous engagements in order to prioritize school as #1 in their lives. I have studied with college men whose purpose is to chase and get women. They love going to the nightclubs and trying to smooth talk a woman into sleeping with them. Once they have accomplished their mission, they discard the woman like a yellow sticky note and begin their search all over again. They are addicted to the chase. College students crave a radical purpose and if they don't find it in Jesus, they will search for it in other areas.

In 2 Corinthians 13:5, Paul says, "Examine yourselves to see whether you are in the faith; test yourselves. Do you not realize that Christ Jesus is in you—unless, of course, you fail the test?" Why would Paul encourage the entire church in Corinth to test themselves, making sure they are in the faith? Doesn't that seem like a really large group of believers to give a test to? Not really. I believe Paul wanted the Corinthians to test themselves because he loved them. Paul was looking ahead to Judgment Day and was asking the Corinthians to do the same thing. He wanted to ensure that they were true Christians. If they were not, it was better for them to discover this now and be able to change as opposed to being surprised on Judgment Day. Don't you agree?

At this time, I would like to follow Paul's example and ask you to test yourself. Since you take exams in school all the time (or at least you used to), test-taking is your normal method of gauging your own knowledge and grasp on a particular subject. I have come up with six questions from Scripture that I want to ask. Only you and God will know the answers. By taking this exam, I hope you realize that Jesus is in you—unless, of course, you fail the test.

TEST QUESTION #1

Have you ever really made Jesus the Lord of your life? If so, is he still your Lord today?

If you confess with your mouth, "Jesus is Lord," and believe in your heart that God raised him from the dead, you will be saved.

—Romans 10:9

Some people try to use this scripture in a watered-down manner to show how easy it is to follow Jesus. "Just believe and say 'Jesus is Lord.' Pretty easy." Are you kidding me?

Can you honestly say, "Jesus is Lord"? Do you understand the definition of the word "lord"? A lord is your master or ruler. In the first century, there were many slaves and therefore many lords. People understood that your lord literally owned you and that you were not to go anywhere or do anything without your lord's permission. In the first century, saying, "Jesus is Lord" had huge implications: You could have your property confiscated by the Roman government, you could be beaten or killed, and your confession could cause your family to be abused. In some cases, children were fed to hungry lions while the parents watched, all because they would not recant their statement that "Jesus is Lord." It was an enormous commitment to say those three words: "Jesus is Lord." It was only said after much prayer and careful consideration.

For most of us, we have never personally experienced having an earthly lord and so this is a foreign concept to us. However, just because slavery has been eradicated in the US, it does not change the definition of the word "lord" and how it was used in the first century. Is Jesus your Lord today? When you think about who you are going to date socially, do you think, "Would Jesus approve of this man/woman?" "Does he/she have the same commitment to Jesus that I have?" If the answer is "No," are you willing to end the relationship? If you really view Jesus as your Lord, then you will choose to date a person who is going to take you closer to God. Do you attend a church where this concept of "lordship" is fully taught and expected of every member? If you do not, are you willing to call your church to repent and even search for a new congregation if they are unwilling? Have you made your decision on which church to attend based in part on its proximity to your house? I surely hope not. If Jesus is truly your Lord, you will have no problem driving a considerable distance to get the encouragement that you need.

Most people want Jesus to be their savior, but I find that not nearly as many people want him to be their Lord. Is Jesus currently the Lord of your life?

TEST QUESTION #2

On a scale of 1 to 10, how zealous are you about learning the Bible?

Now the Bereans were of more noble character than the Thessalonians, for they received the message with great eagerness and examined the Scriptures every day to see if what Paul said was true.

—Acts 17:11

> Let the word of Christ dwell in you richly.
>
> —Colossians 3:16

On Paul's second missionary journey, as he was spreading God's message from town to town, God acknowledged the noble heart of the Bereans over that of the Thessalonians for one main reason: They were eager to read God's word! Some of us have become content to merely listen to the preacher during a sermon and not study the Bible much for ourselves. Even if his sermon is directly from Scripture, God expects us to have a hunger for his word. Are you like the Bereans and have an eagerness to read God's word every day? If not every day, do you at least read the word regularly? Did you start out strong in this area and then lose your zeal over time?

When I first became a Christian in July 1996, I could not wait to read the Bible every day. I began in the New Testament and would make a checkmark in my Bible's table of contents after every book that I read (I still have those checkmarks in my Bible today). I read the entire New Testament within four months and the entire Bible within about one year. Within my first month as a Christian, while I was at nuclear prototype school in Charleston, S.C., I even snuck my Bible into the building through the numerous security checkpoints. I simply wanted more time to study God's word. I was hungry for it. However, after a number of months, I slowly began to lose some of my zeal to read and pray every day. After a while, I had begun to read my Bible only once a week, then once every two weeks. It was not because I didn't want to love God any more; I was just allowing other things to take priority in my life. In other words, I had become "too busy." Can you relate? Not surprisingly, the desires and sins that I was overcoming before were creeping back into my life. I did not even realize it at the time, but Satan was working hard to try to steal my faith...and I was letting him succeed. Eventually, it was a conversation that I had with a Christian brother that helped me to repent.

If we are going to have a great relationship with God and help change the world, we must dedicate ourselves to consistent and fantastic Bible study. For some of us, we must rededicate ourselves.

Let me give you a challenge: If you are not doing well on test question #2, then I urge you to make a commitment right now to read God's word on a regular basis. Also, be sure to tell someone about your decision so they can encourage you and hold you accountable.

TEST QUESTION #3

How much victory are you having with overcoming temptation and sin?

Then Jesus said to them all: "If anyone would come after me, he must deny himself and take up his cross daily and follow me."

—Luke 9:23

So, if you think you are standing firm, be careful that you don't fall! No temptation has seized you except what is common to man. And God is faithful; he will not let you be tempted beyond what you can bear. But when you are tempted, he will also provide a way out so that you can stand up under it.

—1 Corinthians 10:12–13

Jesus tells us in Luke 9 that in order to follow him, we *must* deny ourselves. It does not say that we "should deny ourselves" or that "it would be a good idea to deny ourselves." It is clear that self-denial is an expectation and a requirement. This tells you right away that it will not be easy. In order to follow God, you must understand that God does not take sin lightly. He does not wink at it. He does not smile at it. God feels very strongly about us overcoming our temptations.

Brothers and sisters, is there any sin that is dominating you right now? Let me phrase that differently: Is there any sin that you have made peace with? To make peace with a sin means that you are no longer fighting against it but rather giving in to it regularly. As disciples of Jesus, we can *never* wave the white flag and surrender to our sinful nature. You will never be without sin in your life (1 John 1:8), but we are supposed to master our temptations rather than our temptations mastering us.

You may be tempted to think, "Troy, you don't understand. This is just who I am. For the longest time now, I have been impure or prideful or _____. I cannot overcome it and I feel alone in my struggle." If you have ever been tempted to feel that way, I want you to take courage from 1 Corinthians 10:13, which says, "No temptation has seized you except what is common to man." Translation: You are not the only one. Satan wants us to believe that we are the only one who struggles with a certain temptation, making us believe that we are somehow weird or messed up. That is not true. Everyone has temptations and everyone has sins that they need to overcome. Reading v. 13 further, it says, "And God is faithful." Don't just read over that. That means that God is faithful *to you*! He is with you and wants to help you in your battle. I find that very comforting. The passage goes on to say that God will not let you be tempted "beyond what you can bear," meaning that you will not be unfairly tempted. It will never be a temptation too heavy for you to handle. It is a weight that you can carry. Not only that, but God will give you a way out so that you can overcome. The point: You *can* have victory! That is the power of God! God can take a married couple who fight all the time and make them like two love birds! God can take a person who is ashamed of the gospel and make him or her an evangelizing machine! God can take a person who has struggled with masturbation and impurity for a long time and wash his or her mind totally clean!

How much victory are you having with overcoming temptation and sin? I encourage you to open up to a trusted friend today and talk about this question.

TEST QUESTION #4

On a scale of 1 to 10, how much forgiveness do you show to others?

Then Peter came to Jesus and asked, "Lord, how many times shall I forgive my brother when he sins against me? Up to seven times?"
   Jesus answered, "I tell you, not seven times, but seventy-seven times."
—Matthew 18:21

"For if you forgive men when they sin against you, your heavenly Father will also forgive you. But if you do not forgive men their sins, your Father will not forgive your sins."
—Matthew 6:14

Do you realize that forgiveness is a salvation issue? If we cannot forgive other people when they sin against us, then God will not forgive us when we sin against him. Do you think you will be allowed to enter heaven without God's forgiveness?

I realize that this is a sensitive subject. While everyone has been sinned against at some point in their lives, certain people have seen or experienced things that no person should ever have to go through. I have counseled both men and women who have been sexually abused, physically abused, or emotionally abused. I have counseled people who have seen loved ones murdered before their eyes or witnessed a hurtful divorce. We live in an evil world and much evil has been committed against a lot of people. Despite all of this sin, Jesus still calls his followers to have unconditional love and forgive those who have sinned against them. This is a big calling for some, monumental for others. However, with God's help, it can be done.

The ability to forgive and to love people unconditionally is perhaps Jesus' most amazing quality. During the Lord's Supper, on the night he was to be betrayed by Judas Iscariot, Jesus said, "I tell you the truth, one of you will betray me." The next verse says, "They were very sad and began to say to him one after the other, 'Surely not I, Lord?'" (Matthew 26:21–22). Are you kidding? I find it remarkable that they did not already know who the traitor was. If I knew that someone was going to hand me over to be killed, I would have made it abundantly clear to the room that I had a problem with that person! I do not believe that I could have eaten a meal with a group of men knowing that one of them was my killer and not given anyone a clue. On top of that, he then says, "Surely not I, Lord?" Now he is denying any wrongdoing whatsoever?! He is faking like he is my friend just to fool the group?! My sinful nature would be to jump up and expose him as a traitor. But Jesus was different. He did not get angry. Somehow Jesus was able to forgive Judas without Judas ever asking for forgiveness or showing any signs of repentance. Wow!

This is certainly a high calling, one that I do not write about lightly. If you have been seriously sinned against and have had trouble letting go of the past, l want to encourage you to get counseling on this subject. We cannot allow someone else's sin to define who we are today.

TEST QUESTION #5

Do you allow and feel God's grace in your life?

In him we have redemption through his blood, the forgiveness of sins, in accordance with the riches of God's grace that he lavished on us with all wisdom and understanding.

—Ephesians 1:7

Therefore, there is now no condemnation for those who are in Christ Jesus.

—Romans 8:1

Many of us are guilty souls. We struggle to believe that God has forgiven us of our sins and will allow us to be in eternity with him. Sometimes we even want to be baptized again just to make sure that we were really forgiven. We can easily see how God will allow somebody else to enter heaven, but we struggle with our own salvation because we are keenly aware of our own sins. We need to read Romans 8:1 over and over. We need to memorize it.

If I could ask God one question, I might ask, "Can you help me to better understand your grace?" It is a deep subject that I am learning more about all the time. What I do understand is that God "lavished" his grace upon us. What a descriptive word! It makes me think about my childhood when I used to help my mom bake a cake.

The best part always came at the end when I would try to put as much icing on the cake as I possibly could. I would scrape the inside of the can to get all of the icing out and then *lavish* the icing all over the cake. In that analogy, I want you to realize that you are the cake and God's grace is the icing! We are covered and smothered with God's amazing grace, even if we have a hard time understanding that concept. The good news is that God's grace is not conditional on your understanding of it. He does not lavish it on the Christians who really get it, and only put on a thin layer for those who struggle to understand the meaning of grace.

Having two children has helped me tremendously in my pursuit to understand the depth of God's grace. I have had the privilege of watching Corey and Taylor grow up from birth to ages eleven and nine, respectfully. I have seen them have tremendous victory in learning how to love, share and put the needs of others in front of their own. However, I have also been witness to perhaps thousands of times when they have sinned (anger, pride, selfishness, lying...). Does their sin change the way that I feel about them? Do I love them any less because I witnessed their sinful nature come out again? Absolutely not. I love them unconditionally as my son and daughter. Nothing they ever do will change that. When they sin, my heart is to discipline them and bring them to repentance. However, my immense love for them never wavers. If this is how I love my children, how much more does God love us and show us grace?

TEST QUESTION #6

Are your best friends in God's kingdom or in the world?

> They devoted themselves to the apostles' teaching and to the
> fellowship, to the breaking of bread and to prayer.... All the believers
> were together and had everything in common.... Every day they
> continued to meet together in the temple courts. They broke break in
> their homes and ate together with glad and sincere hearts, praising
> God and enjoying the favor of all the people. And the Lord added to
> their number daily those who were being saved.
>
> —Acts 2:42, 44, 46–47

One of the ways we follow Christ today is by imitating the
faith and lifestyle of those who witnessed Jesus 2000 years ago,
the first-century Christians. What do you notice from Acts 2 about
the relationships between the Christians in the first century? Were
they casual friends or the best of friends? The passage tells us that
they prayed together, hung out together, preached together, ate
together, praised God together and baptized people together. In a
nutshell, they devoted themselves to one another.

What are your friendships like today? Are your best friends
within God's kingdom or are your best friends nonbelievers? I am
not saying that once you become a Christian you need to throw away
all other friendships. Absolutely not. Just the opposite. You want
to maintain those friendships because you need to introduce your
friends to Jesus one day. However, as a Christian, your friendships
with nonbelievers should become different. For example, when I was
in college, I was president of my Lambda Chi Alpha fraternity. Even
though I was not a Christian, I had some really good friends who
cared about me, and we enjoyed a lot of the same activities: playing
basketball and flag football, partying, eating together, hanging
out...but when I became a disciple of Jesus about two years after I

graduated from college, my relationship with those guys began to change. They were still great friends to me, but I was unwilling to do some of the same things that we used to do or talk about some of the same subjects that we used to talk about. They noticed that I had become very committed to God and that I did not talk the way I used to talk. At the same time, I was growing closer and closer with my brothers and sisters in God's kingdom. I felt that I had everything in common with my brothers and sisters in Christ as we worshipped God together, ate together, laughed together, dreamed together, and studied the word together. My best friends quickly became other Christians as I was drawn to their sincerity for God and commitment to his mission.

In my opinion, I believe that the number one reason people walk away from God is lack of spiritual friendships. I always get concerned when I counsel Christians and they do not have best friends within God's kingdom. While everyone in the church cannot be your best friend, you need to have at least five people with whom you can confidently say that you have a deep friendship. When people have fewer than five genuine friendships in the church, that tends to be the threshold for when people struggle spiritually. You may think, "Well Troy, but if my best friends are non-Christians, I will just convert them." Perhaps. But you must understand that's exactly what they will be trying to do to you. I do not mean that they will try maliciously or even intentionally. I am just saying that if Jesus is not first in someone's life, then something else is. And their influence on you could become stronger than your influence on them.

As Paul said, we need to test ourselves. We need to see if we are really in the faith. I gave you six test questions. By no means was this an exhaustive spiritual exam. However, I think it gives you a good beginning into examining where you stand before the Lord. How did you do? Did you find that there were some areas where you have had great success and others areas where you have not? For most of us, we will be strong in some test questions and weak in others. That is expected. However, I hope that by recognizing your strengths and weaknesses you can be both encouraged and challenged to grow in your relationship with Jesus.

Small Group Discussion Questions for Chapter Two

1. Why is the concept of "lordship" confusing to so many people? Are there any areas of your life that you need to commit or recommit to Jesus?

2. Do you believe that a Christian should read God's word regularly? If you read regularly, how has that one simple decision changed your life?

3. What sins are prevalent in the high school, college, or professional world today? How can we overcome them?

4. Do you believe that forgiveness is a salvation issue? Do you currently need to forgive someone? Is there someone whom you have forgiven in the past that you would like to share about?

5. Are you a guilty soul? Do you struggle to understand God's grace in your life? Why or why not? If you had a perfect understanding of God's grace, how would this affect your life?

6. Are your best friends in God's kingdom or in the world? While we are called to have many friends, why would it be important for your best friends to be Christians?

Chapter Three

What's Holding You Back?

"The greatest trick the devil ever pulled was convincing the world he didn't exist. And like that—he's gone."

—*The Usual Suspects*

Do you realize that Satan hates you?! Let that thought sit in your mind for a moment. Even if you don't believe it, it would not change the fact that you have an invisible enemy who hates you and wants nothing more than to hurt you and kill you spiritually. An enemy? Yes, an enemy!

> Your enemy the devil prowls around like a roaring lion looking for someone to devour. Resist him, standing firm in the faith.
>
> —1 Peter 5:8b–9a

Not only does God warn you that Satan is "your enemy," he describes the devil as "a roaring lion." What a frightening comparison! From a physical standpoint, man is no match for a lion. Are you aware that a lion can run up to 65 mph?[8] Crazy, isn't it? We were all in amazement when Usain Bolt from Jamaica won the 100-meter gold medal race at the 2008 Beijing Summer Olympics in a time of 9.72 seconds,[9] setting an Olympic record and becoming the official "fastest man in the world." Had a lion been in that race, he would have crossed the finish line in about three seconds, just as Usain Bolt was hitting the thirty-meter mark. Unbelievable, isn't it? The next time you are driving on the interstate, I want you to look out your window and imagine a lion running beside your car. That will give you a clear reminder of the speed of a lion. Additionally, you must remember that a lion weighs about 500 pounds. That is about twice the size of an American football player. If it so desired, a lion could put two paws against any medium-sized car and turn it over. A lion is a pure carnivore that eats its prey in open fields, generally after sneaking up on its target and killing it in a single bite. Incredibly, of all the millions of animals on this planet, a lion is the animal that God chooses to compare with Satan. That should get our attention.

Make no mistake about it: Satan is your enemy. Do you realize that he has planning sessions in which the entire focus of the meeting is how to take you down? Don't just take my word for it:

Put on the full armor of God so that you can take your stand against the devil's schemes.

—Ephesians 6:11

According to the New World Dictionary, a scheme is "a carefully arranged and systematic program of action for attaining some object or end." Did you know that Satan has a carefully arranged program of action specifically designed to take you out? Scary, isn't it?

Here is what amazes me: Most of the time, people don't even think about the fact that Satan exists. As in the quote from *The Usual Suspects*, Satan's greatest trick is convincing the world that he does not exist. We have an enemy that is so strong, so fast and so wicked, and yet many people go about their daily lives acting as if he really isn't there. While there are many important things to focus on in life like family, school and career, our primary focus needs to be having a deep and meaningful relationship with God. My greatest concern for young people today is that they do not realize the spiritual battle they are in!

While Satan is fast, strong and sneaky, the one thing that he is not is original. Satan does not usually try to tempt us with some new sin that we did not struggle with in the past. On the contrary, he will tempt you with the same sins you have always struggled with, the sins you struggled with in your youth. For example, I have never done drugs in my life. Thus, when I am tempted to sin today, it is not drugs that I struggle with. Rather, it is the impurity, laziness, or selfishness that I struggled with as a younger person.

Ever since the creation of mankind, Satan has been tempting people with the same sins generation after generation: love of self, love of money, greed, jealousy, sexual immorality, anger, drunkenness...how does Satan tempt you? What sin does he dangle in front of you to get you to come down off your cross?

In my decade and a half of leading people spiritually, I have noticed five main things that hold people back from being their best for God.

#1 EXCUSES

We all have them. We don't all use them, but we all have access to them. Too many people use their excuses to justify why they cannot be "sold out" or "totally committed" to the Lord. They say things like:

"I'm too busy."

"My parents or family would not understand."

"I'm too involved in something else right now, but when it slows down..."

"Nobody's open."

"I had some bad things happen to me in my childhood and that is why I am not close to God today."

"I'm not a very outgoing person so I can't share my faith."

Have you ever heard someone use these excuses before? Have you ever used them yourself?

In the parable of the great banquet (Luke 14), a king had prepared a feast and was inviting many guests to come. However, the invited people had all sorts of excuses for not coming.

> "But they all alike began to make excuses. The first said, 'I have just bought a field, and I must go see it. Please excuse me.'
>
> "Another said, 'I have just bought five yoke of oxen, and I'm on my way to try them out. Please excuse me.'
>
> "Still another said, 'I just got married, so I can't come.'
>
> "...Then the owner of the house became angry."
>
> —Luke 14:18–21a

In this parable, the king who is throwing the banquet represents God and the people with all the excuses represent us. Does it seem like God is willing to accept our excuses? While he certainly understands our past and current struggles, God does not want us to use them as reasons why we can't be close to him.

In my experience, there are two kinds of people in this world: people who "make every effort" (Luke 13:24) and people who make every excuse. Which are you?

#2 PROCRASTINATION

Apollo Creed: "He's hooking. He's hooking. He's hooking. Rock, come on! What's the matter with you?"

Rocky Balboa: "Tomorrow. Let's do it tomorrow."

Apollo Creed (screaming): "There is no tomorrow! THERE IS NO TOMORROW! THERE IS NO TOMORROW!"

—Rocky III[10]

Are you a procrastinator? Are you someone who wants to do great things with your life but you think to yourself, "I'll start tomorrow"? Do you tend to put off studying for exams until the last minute or have plans to work out regularly starting tomorrow? If so, then you struggle with procrastination.

Oftentimes, college students have great ambitions and dreams. They have aspirations of being excellent in school, having meaningful quiet times with God and helping to lead many people to Christ. However, the fatal flaw of procrastination sabotages them. I once studied the Bible with a college student at the University of Florida and he seemed pretty interested in following God until we began talking about his sexual relationship with his girlfriend. As I was showing him a scripture about purity (Ephesians 5:3), he looked at me and asked, "Troy, how long did it take for you to give up everything and become a disciple?" "Six days," I told him. I will never forget what he said after that. He looked at me and glibly said, "So you are saying I have six more days to sleep with my girlfriend." I then told him, "If you think like that, you will never have a relationship with God." There is no tomorrow.

It is not just non-Christians who struggle with procrastination. I have counseled many disciples who are lazy and undisciplined.

They have a world of talent but struggle to succeed because they continually put off their responsibilities. They have a hard time saying "No" when they get invited to hang out with friends or are asked to help someone out. They struggle to pay their bills. They consistently stay up too late, causing them to habitually wake up too late. They wait until the last moment to study and then pull an "all-nighter" trying to get ready for an exam or finish a paper. This kind of behavior does not glorify God and will stunt your spiritual growth. These Christians have a bright light, but procrastination is the bowl that hides it, exactly the opposite of what Matthew 5:15 tells us to do.

If you struggle with procrastination, you need to listen closely to Proverbs 12:1, which states that: "Whoever loves discipline loves knowledge, but he who hates correction is stupid." In order to repent and begin living a disciplined lifestyle, you are going to have to want it! You must grow to love discipline. I was not always a very disciplined person, but I have grown to become disciplined because I worked hard at it. If you are serious about growing in this area, here are some ways to do it: First, I recommend that you seek out those whom you recognize as being disciplined and spend time with them. Learn from them and imitate their ways. Second, I recommend that you get a "discipline coach," someone whom you trust that will hold you accountable with such questions as: "What time did you go to bed?" "What time did you wake up?" "Did you attend all your classes?" "Did you arrive on time to work or class?" "Did you meet your spiritual goals?" and "Did you meet all of your financial obligations?" This is serious stuff! Procrastination is one of Satan's biggest weapons to get you to be unproductive in the Lord. If it is not corrected today, you will never be able to change the world tomorrow.

#3 FEAR

Hal Jordan: "The one thing a Green Lantern is supposed to be is fearless. That isn't me."
Carol Harris: "You have the ability to overcome fear!"

—Green Lantern

"Fear is a sickness. It will crawl into the soul of anyone who engages it."
—Apocalypto

Do you remember where the Christians were on the day that Jesus resurrected from the grave? On the greatest day in the history of the world, John 20:19 tells us that: "On the evening of that first day of the week, when the disciples were together, with the doors locked for fear of the Jews, Jesus came and stood among them." Wow! Were the Christians at the grave awaiting Jesus' resurrection? No, they were in a room with the doors locked because they were afraid! They saw what had happened to Jesus and were afraid for their own safety. Even the men and women who walked with Jesus every day for three years still got afraid. I find that encouraging!

Too often I have seen college students have great dreams for God but allow fear to get in the way. They want to start a Bible study group in every dormitory on campus, but they lose heart after meeting one person who opposes them. They begin the semester with great prayers about sharing the gospel with their classmates but then lose faith if the first person is not interested. Unfortunately, fear and discouragement have snatched the godly dreams out of the hearts of many young people.

Often, the anticipation of rejection is worse than rejection itself. When we are thinking unspiritually, we tend to believe that another person will not be open to the gospel and thus reject our invitation. About one week after Kim and I were baptized, our small group (or Bible talk) decided to go to the mall to share our faith. The plan was to split up into groups of two and walk around the mall for one hour and share the gospel and then meet back up to share the victory stories. I was terrified. Interestingly, we all paired up with our spouses, meaning that my partner for the evening was just as young and fearful as I was. Kim and I walked around the mall and stared at all the people walking by, not speaking to a single person. We did this for almost one hour. We were one-week-old Christians and were overwhelmed with fear. Eventually, Kim and I came up with a plan to purchase a shirt so that we could share with the person at the cash register. At least she could not walk away. She had a great response. We were excited that we at least had one story to share with the group.

Have you ever been afraid to share your faith? Have you ever been in a situation when you felt the Holy Spirit prompting you to speak to someone about God but you backed away because you were afraid of what they would think of you? Are there any fears that hold you back today?

Brothers and sisters, we must overcome any fears that we have about standing up for God! Let me remind you of Jesus' words in Luke 9:26 when he says, "If anyone is ashamed of me and my words, the Son of Man will be ashamed of him when he comes in his glory." Have you ever noticed what type of person Revelation 21:8 lists first in describing those who are going to hell? The cowardly. Of all the sinful temptations in my life, I do not want God to view me as cowardly or ashamed of him. Overcoming our fears is not just a good idea; it is required. Please remember that God is patient with us and has given us the Holy Spirit as a comfort and guide. I pray that fear will not hold you back from seeing the radical dreams you have for God's kingdom come true!

#4 COMPROMISE

Jack Bauer: "Nina, you can look the other way once and it's no big deal, except it makes it easier for you to compromise the next time and pretty soon that's all you're doing is compromising, because that's how you think things are done. You know those guys I blew the whistle on? Do you think they were bad guys? Cause they weren't. They weren't bad guys. They were just like you and me, except they compromised, once."

—24, Season 1, Episode 1

When you are dealing with a roommate issue or a spousal problem, compromise is a wonderful thing. However, when you are dealing with God's word and his plan for your life, you must never compromise!

According to the New World Dictionary, to compromise means to choose "something midway between two other things; to make a settlement." Satan tempts us all the time to make a settlement with the Bible by whispering things in our ear like: "No one will ever find out" or "It won't hurt anyone." Thus, we are tempted to relax in our Bible study and prayer or begin watching things on TV or the computer that are inappropriate. We think that our compromise is not hurting anyone, but we fail to realize that our poor decisions are slowly robbing us of our faith and conviction.

One of the reasons we tend to compromise is that we want to fit in or be accepted by others. This desire to look good in someone else's eyes can cause a woman to think, "Well, I can have just one more drink" or "I can probably wear this outfit even though it's a little too revealing." This desire to fit in can cause a man to think, "I can curse just a little bit when I'm around these guys" or "It's OK if I flirt a little with her. After all, she seems to like it." As Christians, we must be resolute in our convictions about wanting to please God and must not give in to peer pressure.

In the first century, Christians were being tempted to give in to peer pressure in numerous ways. One example is when Judaizers (a subset of Jewish Christians) rose up within the church and began teaching that many of the ceremonial practices of the Old Testament, including circumcision, were still binding on the New Testament church. The other Christians were made to feel uncommitted if they did not agree to this militant position, tempting them to compromise their freedom in Christ. Paul addressed this desire to compromise by saying in Galatians 1:10: "Am I now trying to win the approval of men, or of God? Or am I trying to please men? If I were still trying to please men, I would not be a servant of Christ." If you are going to live as a disciple of Jesus Christ, you cannot compromise the word of God for anybody! Do not try to alter your biblical convictions just to fit in to a group or be accepted by another person. In the end, none of those people will be next to you when you stand before God and give an account of your life. If people cannot accept you for who you are as a follower of Jesus, then that is their loss.

#5 DISTRACTION

Satan's number one plan for you is simple: tempt you to leave God. However, if he cannot succeed at plan A, he will simply go to plan B: distract you. There are many Christians today who attend all the services and sing all the songs. They volunteer in the children's ministry or serve as ushers. However, they don't realize that they are distracted from their purpose of loving God with all their heart and are not focused on their mission to seek and save the lost.

It is easy to get distracted. I cannot tell you how many times I have asked Corey, my eleven-year-old son, to go take a shower only to find him a minute later doing something else. "Son, what are you doing?" I will exclaim. "Oh, sorry, Dad," he says. "I was on my way to take a shower but I guess I got distracted."

One of the ways Satan tempts someone to put down their cross is by getting them to focus on something else. Has anything come into your life recently that is taking your focus off of God and his mission? Have you had any problems with your finances, job, relationships or schoolwork that have kept you from seeking God with all your heart? If Satan can get all the Christians to focus their attention on their own lives, then he will succeed in his ultimate goal of preventing the spread of the gospel of Jesus.

Getting the Eye of the Tiger Back

Apollo Creed (speaking to Rocky): "Now when we fought, you had that eye of the tiger, man. The edge! And now you gotta get it back, and the way to get it back is to go back to the beginning. You know what I mean?"

—Rocky III

Do you remember when you first became a Christian? Do you remember how excited you were to wake up each day and read the Bible, anticipating that God was going to say something absolutely incredible to you in your study? What were your prayer times like back then?

When I was a very young Christian, I was so excited to tell others about what I had found in Jesus Christ. I went into the Naval Nuclear School each day hoping and praying to find someone who would be open to a discussion with me about God. The Lord blessed my zeal as I began to have great talks with my friend Ernie. Even though I was very young in the faith, I spoke to Ernie about the things that I knew and soon brought him to an older Christian to help me teach Ernie more adequately about Jesus. Within one month of my own baptism, I had the extreme privilege of baptizing Ernie. When was the last time you prayed to meet an open person whom you could study with and baptize? As Jesus said in Matt 9:37, "The harvest is plentiful but the workers are few." Brothers and sisters, we are the workers! If we are going to change this world for Jesus, we need to have a spiritual edge about us—a zeal to read God's word, pray with all our hearts, be devoted to the body and reach out to the lost.

Does anything hold you back from being your best for the Lord? Do you have a tendency to make excuses? Do you have great dreams that procrastination is sabotaging? Does fear hold you back? Have you begun to compromise God's word in your life? Have you simply become distracted from your purpose of loving God and your mission of saving souls?

Remember that Satan is your enemy. Remember that Ephesians 6:11 tells us that the devil is scheming against you and me, and that his sole mission is to hold you back from being your best for Jesus. Don't allow him to win. Consider what might be holding you back and make a decision to change it today.

Small Group Discussion Questions for Chapter Three

1. What excuses do people use today to justify their lack of total commitment to God? Do you ever use excuses in your life? Explain.

2. Are you a procrastinator when it comes to studying for exams, working out, or accomplishing tasks? How can procrastination negatively affect a person's life? How can a person overcome procrastination and lead a disciplined life?

3. Are there any fears that hold you back today? How can you overcome them?

4. How can a person's desire to "fit in" socially or on the job cause them to compromise? Give an example. Is there ever a right time to compromise?

5. How do you see Satan distracting God's people today? Has anything come into your life recently which could distract you from God's work? How can you overcome it?

Chapter Four

Don't Alter His Altar

"Look man, you can listen to Jimi but you can't hear him. Just because you're listening to him doesn't mean you're hearing him."
—White Men Can't Jump

"Do you understand the words that are coming out of my mouth?"
—Rush Hour

A lot of people seem to be listening to God, but I am not sure that many people are hearing him. If we are all hearing God, then why are there so many different views on what it means to "love God"? Have you ever felt confused by the vast number of different churches in the U.S. who all claim to follow the Bible but have radically different views on what it means to love God? I know I have. Do we really understand the words that are coming out of Jesus' mouth? He said, "If you love me, you will obey what I command" (John 14:15).

What a simple definition—Jesus' definition. If we love God, then we will obey God. The contrapositive of that statement is just as true: If we do not obey God, then we do not love God. With such a clear definition, why do we have so many different standards of

Christianity in today's world?

Too many new age Christians try to alter his altar. What I mean is that too many people try to make the gospel more attractive, as if God needed a facelift. Many have gotten away from preaching the hard-hitting truth that comes directly from the mouth of Jesus and have created their own definition of "loving God." I have heard people say, "I love God, but I just don't go to church" or "I love God in my own way." I have also heard people say, "I know that I'm not giving my best effort right now in following the Lord, but God understands my situation." People tend to create their own image of God to fit the commitment level that they are comfortable with. Even though Jesus says, "Come, follow me" (Mark 1:17), it seems that many people have a tendency to respond by saying, "No, God, you come follow me."

Too many people want to lead the relationship with God instead of letting God lead them. Then they try to rationalize or justify why they are not obeying the Bible in their lives. Imagine I told my son, "Corey, I want you to go rake the yard." He responds by saying, "Sure, Dad" but then goes about his day doing other things and does not actually rake the yard. When I approach him later in the day and question him about it, he says, "Well, Dad, I didn't actually rake the yard, but I did memorize what you said. See: 'Corey, I want you to go rake the yard.' Even more, Dad, I memorized it in the Greek! Aren't you impressed? On top of all that, I called some friends to come over tomorrow and we're going to discuss why you asked me to rake the yard and what the yard would look like if I actually did it." Do you think I would be happy with my son's response? Of course not. However, this is how many people respond to God's commands. Instead of obeying what God's word is clearly telling them to do, they would rather memorize the passage, study the passage in Greek or intellectually discuss its meaning with others. I am not downplaying the importance of memorizing Scripture or discussing the Bible in small groups. On the contrary, those things are of paramount significance in loving God. My point is that God does not want us to do those things in lieu of obedience. When God gives us direction on marriage, dating, purity, serving the poor, evangelizing our city or being devoted to the body, he expects us to do our best to carry out his commands.

Many people have a great interest in wanting Jesus to be their Savior but have little interest in making Jesus their Lord. They want to "live their own way" but be saved in the end nonetheless. This was most apparent to me a few years ago when I went to a UF-Tennessee college football game. I am a big Florida Gator fan and I love going to the games. That day my seat was in the east stands on the 40-yard line, fairly close to the Tennessee marching band. Throughout the first half, two Gator fans sitting two seats away from me were continually yelling obscenities and curse words at the opposing team and their band. It was so bad that I actually switched seats with the girl who was sitting beside me so that she could have a little separation from these two hecklers as she was obviously uncomfortable while sitting next to them. After switching seats, these two men were now directly beside me. They must have screamed 150 curse words at the top of their lungs throughout the first half, with one of the men doing most of the yelling. It was bad. People told them to calm down, but these men just shrugged them off and kept doing it.

I began to pray. I told God that at halftime, when the stadium became quiet and people could actually talk, I was going to try to talk to the main guy that was yelling. When halftime arrived, one of the men went immediately for drinks and I turned to face the main heckler. "Hey, my name is Troy," and I stuck out my hand for a handshake. "Hi, I'm Terry," the man said as he shook my hand. Then I began the speech that I had recited a few times in my mind. "Listen, I'm a Christian and I believe in following Jesus Christ in my life, and it is really difficult for me to enjoy watching this game while you're cursing so much." As I started into my next sentence, he interrupted me with the most far-fetched sentence that I could imagine. "I'm a Christian too!" he exclaimed. I was shocked not only at his words, but at the genuineness with which he said it. He truly believed this about himself! I suddenly felt a mixture of shock and disgust come over me. "Oh, it's on now!" is what I thought in my mind. I looked at him and said, "You're a Christian?" Then I reached down into my pocket and pulled out my small NT Bible, something I carry with me most places (I refer to it as "my dagger"). Now he was shocked. I said "I need to show you a scripture." So we turned to John 8:31–32, which reads: "To the Jews who believed him, Jesus said, 'If you hold to my teaching, you are really my disciples. Then you will know the truth, and the truth will set you free.'"

Then I asked him, "Do you really believe that you're holding to the teaching of Jesus in your life?" He went on to share with me his life story and we had a fantastic Bible study for about fifteen minutes, spanning the rest of halftime. I thought to myself, "What a glorifying moment for God! How many Bible studies are going on in this stadium right now? Praise God!" His friend came back with drinks only to find his buddy studying the Bible with me. I bet that was the last thing he thought he would see upon his return. He just sat beside us quietly and listened. As the second half began, I was eager to see if my new friend would be cursing the same way or if the word of God would change his heart. Amazingly, he only cursed one time in the second half, and that was an accident. The Gators scored a touchdown and on impulse he yelled out a curse word. He actually caught himself in the moment and quickly covered his mouth. That was his only curse word for the rest of the game. God's word is awesome!

This story is an example of how so many people believe that they love God but their lives depict something entirely different. Let's be honest: We all want things easy in life. It's human nature. Have you ever gotten upset because the Internet was slow? It is so frustrating, right? Have you ever searched tirelessly to find the television remote control? We would rather search for twenty minutes than have to get up off the couch to change the channel. Have you ever asked around to figure out which professor is the easiest before taking a class? It's what we do. We like our fast food, texting and diet pills. We prefer our online banking, online classes, and ten-minute workouts. We generally prefer to take the path of least resistance to get to our goal. Do you think this attitude can creep into the church and our approach to Jesus? Absolutely!

As disciples of Jesus, it is our responsibility to use God's word (not our own words) to tell people the story of God and to show his expectations for them. We must use God's word to penetrate the cloud of ambiguity that surrounds the definition of "loving God."

Loving God with All Your Heart

"Teacher, which is the greatest commandment in the Law?"

Jesus replied: "'Love the Lord your God with all your heart and with all your soul and with all your mind.' This is the first and greatest commandment."

—Matthew 22:36, emphasis added

Very simply, Jesus is saying, "Love God with all you've got." What is it about the word "all" that we do not understand? Good athletes give their very best every time they compete. They are not going to make every jump shot or complete every pass, but we expect that they give their *all*. We expect that they show up to every practice, work out with their teammates and try to be the best player that they can be given their talent level. That is all that we can ask for, whether as a teammate, a coach or simply a fan. It is the same with God. God expects that we are doing our best to glorify him— that we are committed to the body and that we read our Bibles and try to apply the Scriptures to our daily lives. Even if we fail (I mean *when* we fail), our graceful God is forgiving, as long as we are really trying.

My favorite time of year is Christmas. Don't you just love Christmas? The lights, the music, the spirit in the air, the time with family—I love it all! Of all the great music, my favorite Christmas song is "The Little Drummer Boy." It is a song about a little boy who plays his drum in front of a king. The song is written through the eyes of the boy. I love the lyric at the end of the song that says: "I played my best for him." A few seconds later the song concludes with: "Then he smiled at me." I love that line—it moves my heart every time! I mean, have you ever heard a little boy play the drums? It is usually not all that impressive. Even if he was amazingly skilled for his age, it would still not be nearly as good as the adult professionals who played before the king regularly. Picture this: a six-year-old child standing in front of an imposing king, playing the absolute best that he can, and the king simply grinning from ear to ear. That picture represents our life before God. It depicts how God feels about you and me when we give our "all" to him.

The Importance of Love

Our love for God must be the motivating factor for everything we do. God makes this very clear in 1 Corinthians 13.

> If I speak in the tongues of men and of angels, but have not love, I am only a resounding gong or a clanging cymbal. If I have the gift of prophecy and can fathom all mysteries and all knowledge, and if I have a faith that can move mountains, but have not love, I am nothing. If I give all I possess to the poor and surrender my body to the flames, but have not love, I gain nothing.
> —1 Corinthians 13:1–4

Do you hear what God is saying, or are you merely listening? Have you ever preached in the language of angels before (what would that even sound like)? Even if you could do that, it would mean nothing if you did it without love. Can you prophecy what is going to happen tomorrow? Do you understand all the mysteries on this planet? Can you move a mountain simply by your faith? Even if you could do any one of these amazing things, it would mean nothing if you did it without love. Have you ever given everything you own to the poor? Would you even consider doing such a selfless act? Are you willing to be a martyr for Jesus by being burned at the stake? Even if you did such amazing things, you would gain nothing if you did them without love.

In God's eyes, love is everything! Our love for God and our love for other people must be what motivates us in our lives.

A Reflection of Jesus

When we decide to love God with ALL of our heart, we become a reflection of Jesus Christ to a lost world. God illustrates this point to us by connecting a glorious moment in the Old Testament with the New Testament. Do you remember the story of Moses when he returned from spending forty days and forty nights with God writing down the Ten Commandments?

> When Moses came down from Mount Sinai with the two tablets of the Testimony in his hands, he was not aware that his face was radiant because he had spoken with the LORD. When Aaron and all the Israelites saw Moses, his face was radiant, and they were afraid to come near him.
>
> When Moses finished speaking to them, he put a veil over his face. But whenever he entered the LORD's presence to speak with him, he removed the veil until he came out.
>
> —Exodus 34:29–30, 33–34

When Moses returned from spending forty days and forty nights with God (without eating bread or drinking water—Wow!), his face was glowing and he did not even know it. What was the Israelites' reaction to this new phenomenon? They freaked out, got afraid. Wouldn't you? Oftentimes in the Old Testament, God would speak directly to one man (Moses, the prophets...) and that one man would communicate to all the others. Today, of course, we have the Scriptures. However, due to the Israelites' reaction, Moses would put a veil on his face when he was with the people but remove it when he was with God.

Amazingly, God is going to use this Old Testament story to describe a Christian in today's world.

> We are not like Moses, who would put a veil over his face to keep the Israelites from gazing at it while the radiance was fading away. But their

minds were made dull, for to this day the same veil remains when the old covenant is read. It has not been removed, because only in Christ is it taken away. Even to this day when Moses is read, a veil covers their hearts. But whenever anyone turns to the Lord, the veil is taken away. Now the Lord is the Spirit, and where the Spirit of the Lord is, there is freedom. And we, who with unveiled faces all reflect the Lord's glory, are being transformed into his likeness with ever-increasing glory, which comes from the Lord, who is the Spirit.

—2 Corinthians 3:13–18

Who is the "we" that Paul is referring to in the first and last sentences of this passage? Answer: the Christians! According to this passage, before we become Christians, a veil covers our faces and blocks our view of the Lord. We only see ourselves, our needs, our problems. However, when we decide to love God and make Jesus our Lord, the Holy Spirit lifts the veil and we can see the beauty of God for the first time. Our eyes get opened to the wonders and the purposes of God. From that time on, we are never again to cover our faces and hide the Lord's glory, the way that Moses did. Instead, we are to live constantly with unveiled faces and reflecting God's radiance to a lost world. Additionally, we are to be transformed more and more into God's likeness every day. How exciting is that?

I love that our calling is to "reflect" the Lord's glory. We are not called to become Jesus himself (because our sinful nature makes that impossible), but rather to reflect him to a dark world. Have you ever tried to look directly into the bright sun? It is pretty difficult, isn't it? No one can do it for very long because your eyes begin to water and they naturally want to close. Injury will occur if you look too long. However, have you ever gazed at a full moon on a dark night? Of course you have. It's beautiful. You can stare at the moon for a long time if you wish. You see, the moon is simply reflecting the light, or glory, of the sun. By itself, the moon is simply a rock with no internal power source. As Christians, we are just like the moon. We have no power source in ourselves. By ourselves, we are really just dust. However, we have the incredible privilege of reflecting the glory of Jesus Christ to everyone around us. Our goal in life is to simply reflect the *Son*.

According to 2 Corinthians 3, people should look at our lives and see Jesus. Not that we are Jesus, but we reflect Jesus. Are you willing to accept this amazing spiritual assignment? Think about it before you answer. If you are going to reflect Jesus, *all of Jesus*, then you cannot come to him and pick out only the things you like. Have you ever gone to a restaurant with a buffet line where you got to pick and choose which foods you wanted and which foods you did not want? Following Jesus is not like that. We cannot go down the spiritual buffet line and say, "I would like some peace please and... oooh, the grace looks really good today. I would like a double helping of grace...but I don't want any of the repentance from sin or the evangelism. No, no; I don't like the way those things taste." When we decide to truly love God, we surrender our lives to him and offer our bodies "as living sacrifices" (Romans 12:1). If we are going to change the world, we must decide as Christians that we are going to reflect ALL of Jesus.

God Does Not Need a Facelift

As I said earlier in this chapter, too many new age Christians try to make the gospel of Jesus more attractive, as if God needed a facelift. They take such biblical commands as "Repent and be baptized" (Acts 2:38) or "Go and make disciples of all nations"

(Matthew 28:18) and offer them as optional in the twenty-first century. Remember, Matthew 28:18–20 is referred to as "The Great Commission," not "The Great Suggestion."

When Peter was preaching the first sermon after the resurrection of Jesus, he was addressing a large crowd in Jerusalem. What a monumental moment in the history of God's people as Peter was now instructing the world on how to enter into a saving relationship with Jesus Christ. He concluded his sermon by saying:

> "Therefore let all Israel be assured of this: God has made this Jesus, whom you crucified, both Lord and Christ."
>
> When the people heard this, they were cut to the heart and said to Peter and the other apostles, "Brothers, what shall we do?"
>
> Peter replied, "Repent and be baptized, every one of you, in the name of Jesus Christ for the forgiveness of your sins. And you will receive the gift of the Holy Spirit."
>
> —Acts 2:36–38

This passage could not be any clearer. If it seems even the slightest bit ambiguous to you, then please go back and read all of Acts 2 so that you can get the full context. According to this passage, in order for someone to receive forgiveness of their sins, they needed to repent of their sins and be baptized in the name of Jesus! Can a person go to heaven without their sins being forgiven? Of course not. This passage gives clear instruction on how to enter into a relationship with Jesus Christ.

However, in my opinion, too many preachers are afraid to preach this message. They are scared that if they teach on controversial subjects like repentance (which means "to change" or "to turn away from") and baptism (which comes from the Greek word *baptizo* which means "to submerge or plunge"), many of their members will become unhappy or leave. You see, many "Christians" today were taught something more convenient called "The Sinner's Prayer." In this new teaching, which started in the 1800s and is not found anywhere in the Bible, a seeker who wants to be saved is to simply pray a prayer, generally led by the preacher at the end of his sermon. In this prayer, you invite Jesus to "come into your heart." The problem with this "new method" of salvation (other than the fact that there is not one person in the Bible who got saved this way) is the fact that it does not call for either repentance or baptism, the very two things that Peter calls all of the first-century seekers to do.

Recently, I was listening online to a sermon by Francis Chan. The sermon was delivered on August 26, 2007 and was entitled "The Holy Spirit, Part 3" (found at www.cornerstonesimi.com). As I was listening to this incredible sermon, I got so excited to hear him take a stand on Peter's teaching about repentance and baptism. Francis Chan had preached the previous Sunday on Acts 2:36–38 and had called his congregation to simply obey what the passage taught. During the next week, he received many phone calls from his parishioners questioning him about his sermon. They said, "It sounded like you were saying I have to repent and then be baptized and then receive the Holy Spirit." They asked, "Can I be a Christian without being baptized?" or "Can I be a Christian without repenting?" or "Can I be a Christian without the Holy Spirit?" Basically, many of the church members were saying, "This is not the way that I came to know Jesus, so what are you saying about my salvation?" When the next Sunday came, he stood before his congregation and described all the questions he was receiving on this subject. He then made an amazing observation, one that I thought was incredibly insightful. He simply looked at his congregation and said, "I want to answer all your questions with a question: Why do you ask? Because they (referring to the first-century seekers) did not ask. When they (pointing to the Bible) heard the gospel message...they asked a different question: 'What do we need to do?' They just did it!... I don't understand where these questions are coming from." What a simple response. Basically, his expectation was that his church needed to obey whatever the Bible taught, even if it was unpopular or went against a previous belief of theirs. I cannot impress upon you how rare this kind of moment is—when a person stands up for the word of God in the face of public disagreement.

The first-century seekers simply decided to do what God was telling them to do through Peter's sermon in Acts 2, which was to repent and be baptized. Is this your conviction? Is this the way that you came to be saved? If not, are you willing to repent of your sins and be baptized to enter into a relationship with God? Are you willing to take a stand on this biblical teaching, even though it goes against some of the progressive teaching of our day?

God's Desire for Your Life

Do you understand that God's desire is to transform you into the likeness of Jesus? That is why God allows both victories and hardships in our lives, in an effort to transform us. However, I believe that at times our tendency is to fight God in this transformation process. Sometimes God tells us to do one thing, but our desire is to do another. A few years ago I took my family to *Epcot Center* in Orlando, Florida with my brother, Jason, and his children, Brian (six) and Brandon (three). When it came time for Jason and his wife, Rachel, to use their fast pass and go on the most popular ride, Soarin', they told Brandon that he was too small for this ride and would stay back with me and Kim. Brandon did not like this idea. He began kicking and screaming as loudly as he could right outside the ride, which also happened to be a very crowded food court area. Kim quickly picked up Brandon and motioned for Jason and Rachel to go ahead to the ride. For the next five minutes, Brandon cried as loudly as he could in Kim's arms. "No! No! No!" is what he kept yelling. People in the food court were staring at us. It was not our most glorious moment. However, Brandon began to realize that he was not going to get his way and needed to obey his father. Within a few minutes, he put his head on Kim's shoulder and soon after fell asleep. Eventually, Brandon submitted to his father's desire and was now at peace. Too often, we are just like my three-year-old nephew, Brandon. We know what our Father is telling us to do, but we refuse to obey it. God is saying to us, "You need to dive into my word every day," but we refuse to obey it. God is saying, "You need to break away from that unspiritual relationship," but we act like we don't hear him. Perhaps God is saying to you right now, "You need to come into the light and uncover the hidden sin in your life" or "You need to repent and get baptized." To paraphrase the quote from *Rush Hour,* "Do you understand the words that are coming out of God's mouth?"

As Jesus said in John 14:15, "If you love me, you will obey what I command." It is so simple. It may not be easy, but it is simple. Too often people invent other definitions of what it means to love God. Too often they do it in order to fit God into their lifestyle. Don't alter his altar. Let's make sure that we define love the way that Jesus does and let's devote our lives to the pursuit of it.

Small Group Discussion Questions for Chapter Four

1. Do you think that people tend to create their own image of God to fit the commitment level that they are comfortable with? Why or why not?

2. Why are there so many different definitions today of the phrase "love God"? Is each one acceptable to God? In the context of Matthew 22:37, what is it about the word "all" that many people have a hard time understanding?

3. What does 1 Corinthians 13:1–4 mean to you?

4. How do you see people watering down the message of Jesus (giving it a facelift) in order to make it more attractive to people? How do you think God feels about this?

5. With 2 Corinthians 3:13–18 in mind, how can you be a reflection of Jesus to others? What part of your character still needs to be transformed in order to be more like Jesus?

Part Two

Change the World

Chapter Five

Pray Like Your Life Depends On It

> Greg Focker: "O dear God, thank you. You are such a good God to us. A kind and gentle and accommodating God. And we thank you, O sweet, sweet Lord of hosts for the smorgasbord you have so aptly lain at our table this day, and each day...by day. Day by day...by day. O dear Lord, three things we pray: To love thee more dearly, to see thee more clearly, to follow thee more nearly day by day...by day. Amen."
>
> *—Meet the Parents*

Sometimes our prayer life is pretty shallow. We can easily get focused on our own needs and not focus on the greater needs that are all around us. People tend to treat God like he is the great Santa Claus in the sky—"I want this.... I need that." Our prayer life can be as if we were a child again who has crawled up into Santa's lap at the mall and we are telling him all the things that we want for Christmas. It is easy to forget that coming before God's throne in prayer is a reverent moment that should be more focused on his kingdom rather than on our own.

My sinful nature is to be self-reliant. If I am not focused on

God, I tend to believe that I can accomplish things in my life through hard work and determination and that I do not need God to get the job done. Oh, I would never say that to anyone. However, when I am not walking closely with God, this must be the message that my life communicates to him. Can you relate?

The real question is: Do you really believe in the power of prayer? Don't just answer "Yes" because that is the good church answer to give. What I am asking is: Does your life show that you really believe in prayer? Let's get real: What did you pray for today? Yesterday? The day before that? Do you consistently have a deep prayer life? Do you pray like your life depends on it?

One of the best examples of the power of prayer is found in the story of Hezekiah. Hezekiah was the king of Judah most known for purifying God's temple and restoring the worship. However, he came to a moment in his life when prayer was the only answer.

In those days Hezekiah became ill and was at the point of death. The prophet Isaiah son of Amoz went to him and said, "This is what the LORD says: Put your house in order, because you are going to die; you will not recover."

—2 Kings 20:1

Remember, in the Old Testament days, God spoke to people through his prophets, and Isaiah was the leading prophet of the day. Isaiah is perhaps the leading prophet of the entire Old Testament. My point is this: When Isaiah shows up at your house and says you are going to die then, my friend, you are going to die! Let's read on...

Hezekiah turned his face to the wall and prayed to the LORD, "Remember, O LORD, how I have walked before you faithfully and with wholehearted devotion and have done what is good in your eyes." And Hezekiah wept bitterly.

Before Isaiah had left the middle court, the word of the LORD came to

> him, "Go back and tell Hezekiah, the leader of my people, 'This is what the LORD, the God of your father David, says: I have heard your prayer and seen your tears; I will heal you. On the third day from now you will go up to the temple of the LORD. I will add fifteen years to your life.'"
>
> —2 Kings 20:2–6

Hezekiah was told by Isaiah (who was speaking the very words of God) that he was going to die. However, because he prayed and was a righteous man, God decided to change his original plan and allow Hezekiah to live another fifteen years. This is the power of prayer!

When was the last time you wept as you prayed? Tears show that you are desperate. Tears show that you have nowhere else to turn. Tears show that perhaps you have tried to change this thing on your own, only to encounter failure over and over again. When you cry in your prayers, it comes from the recognition that God is everything, you are nothing, and that only by the hand of God can this situation be changed.

In July 2008, my wife and I were asked to speak at the International Campus Ministry Conference being held in Baton Rouge, Louisiana. It was amazing, as 1800 college students came together to hear the word of God and to help rebuild the Lower Ninth Ward of New Orleans, a place that was devastated by Hurricane Katrina. It was an amazing day of service by the largest single group that has ever volunteered to rebuild New Orleans. As Kim and I were vacationing the week before the conference, my son, Corey, who was seven years old at the time, fell from the staircase at the house we were renting. Since the staircase had no side railing, he literally fell off the side of the staircase from a height of about ten feet and landed on the hard tile below. He landed on his head and back. As a parent, you generally know your child's cry—many times I had heard his hungry cry, tired cry or even injury cry. However, this cry was unlike anything I had ever heard before. After hearing a "thud!" in the room next to me, Corey immediately let out a scream full of pain, fear and panic. We rushed in to find his body contorted under the staircase, temporarily unable to move. We quickly dialed 911 and had an ambulance at our place within five minutes. By this time, Corey had a bump on the back of his head that had swelled to the size of a golf ball...then a baseball...and now a softball. It just kept growing. The paramedics tried to put a neck brace on him, but the bump was so large that the brace would not fit. Thus, they had to cut out part of the neck brace with some scissors (a difficult task to do) so that it would fit around my son's bump. This all happened so fast. Everyone was in hysterics. Kim and I were both crying yet trying to stay strong so that we could communicate with the paramedics and make the right decisions. When they placed my son on a stretcher and put him in the ambulance, Kim climbed in as well to ride with him. I jumped into the passenger seat of my brother's car, and he drove me to the hospital behind the ambulance.

It was at that point that my emotions began to really hit me. I realized that my son was seriously injured—that he could die or have brain damage from this fall that could affect him for life—and there was absolutely nothing in my power that I could do about it. It was all in the hands of God! As my brother drove the car, I began to cry out to my God to rescue my son. I *begged* God with tears to heal Corey from this head injury. There was nothing else I could do. There was nowhere else I could turn. I was helpless and desperate...and my prayer showed it. Amazingly, God answered my prayers! After numerous tests, Corey was found to be healthy. The only physical reminder that Corey has today is a small bump that still remains on the back of his head. When Kim and I showed up at the campus conference the next week, this story and subsequent answered prayer was all we wanted to talk about. Since Kim was teaching a class on grace, she threw out her entire lesson and rewrote it based on Corey's fall. After all, it was the best lesson on grace we had ever witnessed personally.

Three days after Corey's fall, once he was back in our rental house (a newly rented house that did not have a deathly staircase in it), my entire family went to the fire station that had answered our distress call. Amazingly, all of the heroes who rescued my son were in the fire station that day. It was a celebration! To quote the song "Celebration" by Kool and the Gang: "There's a party goin' on right here. A celebration to last throughout the years." (OK, so that makes me look old.) We spent a while at the fire station that day, just getting to know the firemen. We simply wanted to say "Thank you" for what they did and show them how God had answered our prayers. At the end, the firemen allowed us to climb on top of the fire truck and ride around the block. I will never forget that time, especially how God answered my prayer.

People Might Think I'm Crazy

Too often as Christians, our prayers are safe. We pray for good health, safe travels on a particular journey, protection for our family or children, rescue from financial problems, and so on. I am not saying it is wrong to pray for safety, but if we are not careful, we can become obsessed with safe passage through this life.

I believe one thing that really gets God excited is to see his children praying crazy, radical prayers. Many people pray generic prayers. God must hear so many of those. When was the last time you prayed something radical? What I mean is this: When was the last time your prayers fired up God and scared you at the same time? Instead of praying, "God, make me a humble man," are you willing to pray, "God, please do *whatever it takes* to make me humble"? Instead of praying "God, I want to grow closer to you this semester," pray "God, please do *whatever it takes* to help me grow closer to you." That's scary, isn't it? Have you ever prayed "God, please use me to convert at least one person in each of my classes this semester"? Are you willing to pray, "God, I am going to share my faith with whomever I sit next to on the bus today. Please lead me to the right seat"? I believe God gets so excited to see his children praying radical prayers and then walking by faith. As God says in Jeremiah 32:27, "I am the Lord, the God of all mankind. Is anything too hard for me?"

When was the last time you thought, "If I tell someone else that I prayed this, people are going to think I'm crazy!" This occurred in my life a few months ago, as a married couple in my church was going through some serious marital problems and the wife (let's call her Teresa) decided that she wanted to divorce her husband. Even though she had two small children and no biblical grounds for divorce, she decided that she no longer wanted to be a Christian, would no longer attend church and wanted to live a wild lifestyle of drugs and partying (this was her life before becoming a Christian while in college). Furthermore, she informed all the Christians to no longer call her or come to her house, as her mind was made up. My heart sank. I loved Teresa and her husband very much and had known them for over a decade. What could I do at this point? One day I was in my bedroom, and I was on my hands and knees crying out for this couple, especially for Teresa. As tears were streaming down my face, I felt as though God was putting a message on my heart that I needed to say to Teresa. My heart was burning and it led me to pray a radical prayer. I knew not to call her or go to the house, since she explicitly asked for no one to do this. So I prayed, "God, please let me run into her—somehow, some way. If you will let me run into her, then I will tell her the three things you want me to say." Since faith and deeds must go hand-in-hand, I devised a crazy plan: I decided that I would drive to the grocery store on her side of town and go inside for twenty minutes. I would push a cart up and down each aisle but would not purchase any items. If she showed up, I would tell her what God had put on my heart to say to her. If she did not show, I would simply put my cart away and drive home. However, I was certain that she would be there. Even though I had no way of knowing if this was actually the grocery store that she even shopped at and I knew my odds were about one in a million, I had faith in God, not in my plan. Since I had an opening in my schedule that day from about 1:00 to 3:00 p.m., I decided that was when I would go. I kept praying all day about it, excited to watch what God was going to do. However, I also kept thinking, "People are going to think I'm crazy for praying this prayer. What if she isn't there? Will I ever tell anyone that I did this?"

When 1:00 p.m. came, I began the approximately thirty-minute drive to the grocery store on the other side of town, a store that I never go to due to its location. On the way there I stopped for gas. That actually messed with my head as I began to wonder, "Did the five minutes that I just spent getting gas throw this whole plan off? Perhaps Teresa would have been at the store but now she won't because I stopped." It is amazing how Satan tempts us to continually doubt, even in our most faithful of times. However, I just kept praying and drove on to the store.

When I arrived in the parking lot, I prayed one more time in my car and then stepped out to walk inside. I grabbed a grocery cart and literally took *one* step inside the store when I saw Teresa! My heart began racing! She was right at the entrance to the store looking at an item. Immediately, her eyes met mine. She continually stared at me as I walked over to her. When I got to her, my heart was beating so fast that my first words to her were actually, "Give me a second. I'm out of breath." I could barely breathe! I felt like I had just run three miles! I knew in that moment that God had just answered my prayer and I was about to speak to Teresa a message that was directly from the Lord. I was overwhelmed. I explained to Teresa about my prayers for her and that the only reason I came to that grocery store that day was to speak to her the words that God had put on my heart. Her jaw dropped to the floor when I said that. I then told her: "I have three things that I believe God wants me to say to you: Number one: God loves you! God loves you so much and he wants you to know that. Number two: You need to repent! The sins that you are now committing are wrong and you need to change immediately. Number three: Remember the cross! I don't want you to come back to God because of the church, your friends, or your children. You need to return to God because of the fact that Jesus died for your sins. Let that be your motivation." Tears began to stream down her face. We spoke for a few more minutes, she agreed to talk to me more via email, I put away my empty grocery cart, and I went back to my car. Once inside my car, I threw my arms over my steering wheel and began to loudly praise God with tears rolling down my face! In all of my years as a preacher of God's word, never before had I felt God speak through me more clearly than he did that day.

God wants us to pray like our life (or someone else's life) depends on it...because it does! Does it truly bother you when you see someone, especially a friend, making wrong choices and walking down the wide road to destruction? Have you ever cried or fasted for someone's salvation? You should. Have you ever had tears roll down your face as you prayed for God to change something in your own character or to give you repentance over a sin that continually defeats you? You should. God wants us to understand that he is the Creator of this world and that he can do *absolutely anything!* I believe when a Christian begins praying for radical things to happen, God is on his throne exclaiming, "Finally! Someone down there gets it!"

Two Obstacles to Prayer

1. Humanism

Sometimes as Christians, *we become self-reliant* and we believe that we have some kind of power to change a situation. That is one reason why a Christian might not pray with passion and desperation. We honestly think that we can do it without God. While we may never admit that, our lack of passionate prayer shows that we really believe it. Do you really want to help someone become a Christian? Do you really want to have a pure dating relationship? Do you really want to overcome your lack of discipline so that you can do better in school? Do you really want God to give you repentance with a particular sin that has plagued you for a long time? If so, then you have to pray about it. I am not talking about the kind of prayer where you frequently get distracted or your mind wanders off to another thought. I am talking about on your knees, face in the carpet, heartfelt cries to the only person who can rescue you: the Creator of the world.

> They devoted themselves to the apostles' teaching and to the fellowship, to the breaking of bread *and to prayer*.
>
> —Acts 2:42, emphasis added

In the first century, prayer was not just the focus of the apostles. Prayer was the focus of anyone who called themselves a Christian.

In the first century, prayer was both spontaneous and contagious. As disciples hung out together, they prayed together. It was simply who they were and was a part of their way of life. They were not trying to win the world on their own strength, nor was their faith simply in their leaders or their church. They realized that the only way to become like Jesus and to spread the gospel around the world was to be dependent on God through prayer.

Humanism can easily creep into our church. We can easily begin to rely on our gifts and the gifts of others instead of relying on the power of God. As Christians, we must realize that the mission in front of us is overwhelming and impossible...without God. Whether we are alone or meeting with a group, let's make a focused effort to constantly pray.

2. Doubt

Perhaps you realize that it will take the power of God to change a situation in your life and you truly believe that God can do anything. However, you doubt that God would really do it for you. You think to yourself, "I know that God can grant amazing requests from other people, but I just don't think he's gonna do it for me." If you grew up not being very close to your earthly father, you may struggle to "feel" close to God today. You may wonder if he really wants to rescue you or if he even hears your prayers. If you feel this way, I want you to listen closely to the message of the parable of the persistent widow.

> Then Jesus told his disciples a parable to show them that they should always pray and not give up. He said "In a certain town there was a judge who neither feared God nor cared about men. And there was a widow in that town who kept coming to him with the plea, 'Grant me justice against my adversary.'

"For some time he refused. But finally he said to himself, 'Even though I don't fear God or care about men, yet because this widow keeps bothering me, I will see that she gets justice, so that she won't eventually wear me out with her coming!'"

And the Lord said, "Listen to what the unjust judge says. And will not God bring about justice for his chosen ones, who cry out to him day and night? Will he keep putting them off? I tell you, he will see that they get justice, and quickly. However, when the Son of Man comes, will he find faith on the earth?"

—Luke 18:1–9

Did you get the point of this parable? The simple message is this: As Christians, we need to continually pray to God and never stop. That is what he wants in a relationship with us. Since God is the Great Judge, he gives us a story about a worldly judge, a person with all authority to grant requests. However, he doesn't even care about people. This worldly judge is depicted as a person who only cares about himself and even grants requests just so that a person will leave him alone. Such is the depth of his selfishness (an obvious contrast to the large heart and intense love that God has for his people). God uses this illustration to show that if a bad judge will grant requests to the constant seeker, how much more will the Righteous Judge grant requests. We must understand: God wants us to "cry out to him day and night." God wants to be your Great Rescuer when you have nowhere to turn.

Perhaps the best part of this parable is also the most subtle one. Did you notice what type of person God uses to depict the Christian (you and me) in this story? A widow. Why would God choose a widow to represent you and me? Why not choose a young child, which would represent the future generation and someone who could change the world? Why not select a spiritual leader, someone who would represent the current church and our need for "influential" men and women to pray? No, God chooses a widow. How do you think a widow was viewed in the first century? They were insignificant. They were a group that needed to be taken care of because, often, they could not care for themselves. In Acts 6:1, when food was being distributed to the widows, the Grecian widows were being overlooked. Even when taking care of the poor, some widows still got passed by. This shows the societal view on such a helpless group. Is it simply a coincidence that God chooses a widow to represent you and me in this story? Not at all. I think God is sending a message to everyone who is tempted to believe that they are insignificant or that their prayer request is not important enough to garner God's attention. If you struggle with these thoughts, then God is trying to send you a simple message: *"You are important to me! I want to hear your prayers! I want to answer your prayers!"*

I believe the last line of this parable is of paramount importance. When Jesus returns, will he find faithful Christians? Will he find men and women who have persevered through their trials, through their past, and through their insecurities to continually put their faith in him? That is what God wants to see in us. The question is: Does he see it? Does God see a plethora of faithful Christians today who rely on him in prayer? Does he see it in you?

Staying Organized in Prayer

One of the tools that I use to help me stay focused and disciplined in my prayer life is a Prayer Sheet. It follows the instructions given by Jesus in Matthew 6:9–13 on how to pray. It may help you to stay disciplined and organized in your prayer life.

Prayer Sheet

"This then, is how you should pray."

"Our Father in heaven, hallowed be your name."

Attributes of God

Self-existence	Holiness	Omniscience
Self-sufficiency	Faithfulness	Omnipotence
Eternity	Grace	Majesty
Wisdom	Love	Beauty
Justice	Forgiveness	Might
Mercy	Goodness	Glory
Sovereignty	Perfection	

Names of God

"The Lord is my shepherd." Psalm 23:1

"The Lord Will Provide" Gensis 22:14

"The Lord Our Righteousness" Jeremiah 23:6

"God Most High" Genesis 14:18-20

"The God who sees me" Genesis 16:13

"I am" Exodus 3:14

"Your kingdom come, your will be done on earth, as it is in heaven."

The Kingdom

Your dreams

Every nation

Harvest

Workers

The lost

Other sister churches

Your Local Church

Elders	Middle School Ministry
Evangelist	High School Ministry
Deacons	Community service
Marrieds Ministry	Chemical Recovery
Campus Ministry	Kingdom Kids
Singles Ministry	Build family

Gone/Not Forgotten	Sick	Friends/Neighbors	Family Members
1.	1.	1.	1.
2.	2.	2.	2.
3.	3.	3.	3.
4.	4.	4.	4.
5.	5.	5.	5.

"Give us today our daily bread."

Church Requests	**Gratitude**	**Personal Requests**
Bible Talks/small groups	Salvation	1.
Non-Christian spouses	The church	2.
Finances	God's kingdom	3.
Raising up leaders	The Bible	4.
Strong marriages	Material blessings	5.
Dating couples	Bible Talk (each person)	6.
Student's grades	The cross	7.
Young disciples	Heaven	8.
Mentoring	Past/Future victories	9.

"Give us today our daily bread."

Challenging Sins (1 Tim. 3:1-5)	**Challenging Sins (Gal. 5:19)**
Lovers of self, Unholy	Sexual immorality, Fits of rage
Lovers of money, Without love	Impurity, Selfish ambition
Proud, Unforgiving	Debauchery, Factions
Disobedient to parents, Slanderous	Idolatry, Envy
Ungrateful, No self-control	Hatred, Drunkenness
A form of godliness, but denying its power	Jelousy, and the like...

"Lead us not into temptation, but deliver us from the evil one."

Following the Holy Spirit	**Delivery from Satan**
Surrender	Victory over Satan's attacks
Current or future job	Rescue from our trials
Current for future boyfriend/girlfriend	Perseverance
Current or future roommates	
Praying before an event (proactive faith)	

If we are going to change the world, the first thing we must do is pray like our life depends on it. Nothing will ever happen to change this world outside of the power of God. Before we can move on, we must all have a deep conviction about the necessity for radical prayer.

Small Group Discussion Questions for Chapter Five

1. Do you believe in the power of prayer? Does your prayer life support your answer?

2. What are some of the most important prayer requests that you currently have right now? Do you pray often to God about these things?

3. Which of the scriptures in this chapter (or other passages not used here) encourage you the most in your prayer life? Why?

4. What are some answered prayers that God has given you in the past?

5. I spoke about two obstacles in our prayer life: humanism and doubt. Do you struggle with either of these?

6. Do you use a prayer sheet to help you stay organized in your prayer life? How could the prayer sheet found at the end of this chapter help you?

Chapter Six

Living on the Wrong Side of Easter

"There is a brotherhood between us. If you're not willing to give up everything, you've already lost."

—*Act of Valor*

Most people are not willing to give up everything for Jesus. They value their "things," their time or their lives too much to give up everything for God's kingdom. They are content with being lukewarm and even warn others not to "go overboard with religion." What they do not realize is that giving up everything is a requirement for passage into God's eternal home.

"In the same way, any of you who does not *give up everything* he has cannot be my disciple."

—Luke 14:33, emphasis added

What Does It Mean to "Live on the Wrong Side of Easter"?

While I understand that the word "Easter" is a secular term, I use it here because the world today associates this word with the three days ranging from Jesus' death on Friday to Jesus' resurrection on Sunday. If we are going to change the world, the sacrifice of Jesus *must inspire every Christian to give up everything!* Only then do we share a brotherhood that can change the world!

I am convinced that too many people live on the wrong side of Easter. What I mean is that they tend to live on Friday rather than on Sunday. Many people, even some who call themselves Christians, live as though Jesus is still dead. The same power that resurrected Jesus from the grave is not evident in their lives. Too many people view God as a killjoy, as a Creator who invented all these fun things to do in life but then calls his followers to abstain from all of them. They believe that God wants his people to lead boring lives today in order to receive the promise of heaven tomorrow. They do not understand God's incredible love and that he makes this life-changing power available to us all. They do not understand that the Christian life is designed to be the most exciting life of all—life to the full (John 10:10)!

In my opinion, one of the most heart-wrenching, tearful movies of all time for any Christian has to be *The Passion*, directed by Mel Gibson. What an amazing film! I arranged for my entire congregation to see it together in the theater when it first came out in 2004, as did many other churches and religious groups. While I was so grateful to see the cross of Jesus depicted so biblically on the big screen, I was also saddened to see that the two-hour, six-minute film was almost entirely focused on the death of Jesus. When the movie concluded, I thought to myself, "Why did you end it there? You have not told the best part. You have not told the good news of the resurrection!" The entire reason that Jesus' death is so important is because *he resurrected from the grave* three days later, just as he said he would! How could someone make such an amazing movie about such an important subject and leave that part out?!

There needs to be a sequel movie where Jesus rises from the grave, appears to the 500, shows the many convincing proofs that he is alive, and ascends into heaven! Sadly, that movie has not yet been made. How tragic! It is simply another reminder to me of how too many people live on the wrong side of Easter.

Did you know that the event that changed this world more than any other single event in history is the resurrection of Jesus Christ? I am not trying to be sensationalist; I am merely stating a fact. Jesus' resurrection is the most important event in the history of the world! It is the one event that changed the lives of our first-century brothers and sisters, and it propelled their message around the world. Consider the events of the day of Jesus' resurrection:

> On the evening of that first day of the week, when the disciples were together, with the doors locked for fear of the Jews, Jesus came and stood among them and said, "Peace be with you!" After he said this, he showed them his hands and side. The disciples were overjoyed when they saw the Lord.

—John 20:19

When Jesus resurrected on Sunday morning, where were his disciples? Were they gathered at the tomb in celebration, anxiously waiting for Jesus to come back to life as he had prophesied about earlier? No, they weren't. Instead, they were gathered in someone's house *with the doors locked* because they were afraid that what had just happened to Jesus would now happen to them as well. After he had walked with and taught these disciples for three years, this lack of faith could have been a devastating blow to Jesus' ministry. However, I love that Jesus' first four words were not, "I am so disappointed" or "You of little faith." Instead, Jesus says, "Peace be with you!" Don't you just love Jesus' compassion and patience? As David prays in Psalm 86:15, "But you, O Lord, are a compassionate and gracious God, slow to anger, abounding in love and faithfulness." These great qualities of God are seen very clearly on the evening of Jesus' resurrection.

As I consider this scene with the disciples fearfully locked behind closed doors, what strikes me is that they had already heard the teachings of Jesus, seen the numerous miracles, and even witnessed the death of Jesus on the cross. However, *none of those things* motivated them to unlock their doors. *None of those things* ignited the flame of evangelistic zeal that we witness throughout the book of Acts. The moment that changed their lives forever was when Jesus walked in the room (with the doors still locked—how cool!). At that moment, when the disciples saw the resurrected Jesus, they basically said, "This changes everything!"

The unequivocal message of the first-century church was that Jesus Christ had risen from the dead! Consider the following samples taken from just the first four chapters of the Book of Acts (all emphasis added):

> After his suffering, he showed himself to these men [the apostles] and gave many convincing proofs *that he was alive.*
>
> —Acts 1:3

> (Peter speaking) "Therefore it is necessary to choose one of the men who have been with us the whole time the Lord Jesus went in and out among us, beginning from John's baptism to the time when Jesus was taken up from us. For one of these must *become a witness with us of his resurrection.*"
>
> —Acts 1:21–22

(Peter speaking) "This man [Jesus] was handed over to you by God's set purpose and foreknowledge; and you, with the help of wicked men, put him to death by nailing him to the cross. But God *raised him from the dead*, freeing him from the agony of death."

—Acts 2:23–24

(Peter speaking) "Seeing what was ahead, [David] spoke of *the resurrection of the Christ*, that he was not abandoned to the grave, nor did his body see decay. *God has raised this Jesus to life*, and we are all witnesses of the fact."

—Acts 2:31–32

(Peter speaking) "You disowned the Holy and Righteous One and asked that a murderer be released to you. You killed the author of life, but *God raised him from the dead*."

—Acts 3:14–15

The priests and the captain of the temple guard and the Sadducees came up to Peter and John while they were speaking to the people. They were greatly disturbed because the apostles were teaching the people and *proclaiming in Jesus the resurrection of the dead*.

—Acts 4:1–2

(Peter speaking) "If we are being called to account today for an act of kindness shown to a cripple and are asked how he was healed, then know this, you and all the people of Israel: It is by the name of Jesus Christ of Nazareth, whom you crucified but *whom God raised from the dead*, that this man stands before you healed."

—Acts 4:9–10

> All the believers were one in heart and mind. No one claimed that any of his possessions was his own, but they shared everything they had. With great power the apostles *continued to testify to the resurrection of the Lord Jesus,* and much grace was upon them all.
>
> —Acts 4:32–33

Do you get the point? The message of the first-century church was that Jesus Christ rose from the dead. That is what they believed, that is what they preached, and that is what they eventually died for. Even as Paul shares his Acts 9 conversion story in Acts 22 and 26, what is the focus of his testimony? That Jesus appeared to him.

Throughout the book of Acts, as Paul and other disciples were starting churches in other cities, their central message was that Jesus rose from the dead and they are eyewitnesses of this fact. Therefore, this proves that Jesus is the Christ and you should put your faith in him.

**If the resurrection of Jesus Christ is not true,
nothing in life matters!**

**However, if the resurrection of Jesus Christ is true,
nothing else matters!**

Is the resurrection of Jesus a big focus in your life? Is it the motivation behind why you live as a Christian today? If so, then let me ask you a hypothetical question: If an archeologist somehow discovered the bones of Jesus in an ancient grave tomorrow and could now prove that Jesus was a phony (obviously, this is not going to happen), what would change in your life? For most people, nothing would change. Even for many people who call themselves Christians, they would still wake up the next day, have breakfast, go to work, and continue to live the same "good lives" that they have always lived. Outside of the extra two hours they would now have on Sunday mornings, nothing would really change. But for a true disciple, everything would change! Your purpose of loving God, your mission in saving souls, your marriage, your choice in friends, your depth with friends, your dating relationship, your devotion to church, how you look at money, your dependence on prayer, your time studying the Bible...all of this would change in an instant because the foundation of your life had been based on a lie.

> And if Christ has not been raised, our preaching is useless and so is your faith.... And if Christ has not been raised, your faith is futile; you are still in your sins. Then those also who have fallen asleep in Christ are lost. If only for this life we have hope in Christ, we are to be pitied more than all men.
>
> —1 Corinthians 15:14, 17

You see, the resurrection is everything! If it really did not happen, then Christians are the most pitiful group in the world. If it really did not happen, then we are still not saved and our forefathers who died in Christ are actually lost. However, since there were so many witnesses to the resurrection in the first century, they knew that it was true. Therefore, they preached about it with boldness and conviction. Are you truly convinced about the fact that Jesus resurrected? If so, then it has to change your life!

> For Christ's love compels us, because *we are convinced* that one died for all, and therefore all died. And he died for all, that *those who live should no longer live for themselves* but for him who died for them and was raised again.
>
> —2 Corinthians 5:14–15, emphasis added

Reel In the Real Him

When a person is willing to let go of their sin and connect with the message of the cross, their life changes radically. They transfer from the darkness to the light and begin to live a life of great impact. Here are some stories of college students from our Gainesville Christian Church campus ministry who were willing to reel in the real him:

Alex Forges and Jon Sherwood

From 1999 to 2003, I had a Haitian college student in my church named Alex Forges. Alex was one of our main student leaders at Santa Fe Community College, and we had a Paul/Timothy relationship together where I mentored him every week. Alex was fired up for God. At the beginning of one semester, he made a personal goal to share a scripture with at least one person every day. Each day he would carry his Bible onto campus and find one person to share a passage with. He asked me to hold him accountable every week to this goal. Every week I asked him about the goal and almost every week he was able to respond "seven for seven." Amazing!

One day Alex was in the SFCC computer lab wearing his Christian Student Association (our campus club) T-shirt. A non-Christian friend named Jon Sherwood, who had previously noticed that Alex never cussed or complained, had quietly been watching Alex to see if he would mess up. Jon noticed the shirt and went up to him and said, "That's a cool shirt. Where can I get a shirt like that?" Alex responded by saying, "You can't wear this shirt. You have to change your life in order to wear this shirt." Alex began telling Jon about the Bible and shared about how the resurrection of Jesus had changed his life. Alex went on to describe how his dating relationship with his girlfriend, Melissa, was completely pure because of it. He had been dating Melissa for two years and had never had sex with her. Jon responded to Alex's story by saying, "That's impossible! You must be lying! Nobody has a relationship with a girl in college without having sex." Alex responded by saying, "I treat her like my sister in Christ." Jon thought he was crazy and concluded that something must be wrong with Alex! Over the next few weeks, Jon began studying the Bible with Alex and some other disciples in order to learn more about the real Jesus. Having been abused as a young child and later addicted to drugs, Jon was searching for the truth about life and our purpose here on earth. He found answers to all his questions in the life of Jesus. Eventually, I was brought into the Bible studies and, within a few days, Jon became a Christian and was baptized into Christ! A Haitian and a white guy went on to become best friends and help teach the word of God all over Santa Fe College. Alex eventually married Melissa and, a few years later, they went on to serve in the full-time campus ministry in the South Florida Church of Christ. Jon went on to graduate from SFCC and then graduate from the University of Florida. He eventually served as a campus minister with us in Gainesville and went on to lead his own pure dating relationship with a great sister named Brittany Wright. Jon and Brittany are now married and both serve in the full-time campus ministry in Tallahassee, Florida.

Ian Scott

One of the most talented young men I have ever had the privilege of studying the Bible with is Ian Scott. Ian grew up here in Gainesville in a loving family who went to church regularly and had consistent family Bible devotionals. From a young age, Ian learned about God and how to do the "right things" and stay out of trouble. However, as he got older, Ian became more concerned about doing the "right things" than what was really going on in his heart. By the time he reached high school, he had allowed the word of God to be something that he knew about rather than something that he desired to be a real part of his life.

I first met Ian when he was seventeen years old and a senior in high school. He was 6' 3", 310 pounds and was a high school All-American in football as a defensive tackle. He was being heavily recruited by most major universities around the country and had numerous scholarship offers. Additionally, he was the starting center on his high school basketball team, which had won back-to-back state titles during Ian's junior and senior years. On top of all that, Ian was the valedictorian of his 500-member high school senior class. Talk about impressive!

As we began having individual Bible studies, I noticed that Ian had a lot of Bible knowledge but had very little faith. I challenged him to begin reading the Bible every day, which he embraced. One day we (John Hoyt, Joe Bruno, Ian and I) were studying the Bible together on the bleachers of the UF football stadium—perhaps the most inspiring place for a Bible study in Gainesville. We looked at scriptures about discipleship and what it means to truly make Jesus your Lord. As Ian asked questions and wrestled with this concept, I will never forget what he said to me. "Troy, the Scriptures are saying that I have to be 100% devoted to Jesus. However, when I get to UF, I will also have to be 100% devoted to football and 100% devoted to my schoolwork as a mechanical engineering student. That is 300%. I can't do that." Through the leadership of the Holy Spirit, I showed him Mark 10:27 where Jesus says, "With man this is impossible, but not with God; all things are possible with God." After much prayer, Ian decided to radically change his life. He broke up with his longtime girlfriend, Crystal, so that he could focus more on his relationship with God and was baptized on April 7, 2000. Crystal, who was already studying the Bible with my wife and some other sisters, also became a disciple a few weeks later. Ian went on to play football at the University of Florida, starting at defensive tackle his sophomore and junior seasons and earning numerous accolades. Along the way, he maintained a 4.0 GPA in engineering and was able to study the Bible with many of his football teammates as he led a weekly Bible study group for those within the athletic department.

Throughout his three years in college, Ian helped to convert three of his football teammates as well as many other UF college students. After three football seasons, he decided to enter the NFL Draft early as well as marry his once-again girlfriend, Crystal. He was drafted by the Chicago Bears and went on to be a starting defensive tackle in the NFL. Ian even got to play in Super Bowl XLI, when the Bears played the Indianapolis Colts. He played in the NFL for seven seasons and also had the privilege of speaking at numerous campus and teen events around the country. Ian and Crystal are now living back in Gainesville, Florida and are raising their four children. They both still lead a weekly Bible study group in their home as well as lead our church in community service, heading up our Gainesville chapter of *HOPE worldwide*.

Katie Indarawis

One of the most vibrant and charismatic young women I have ever met is Katie Indarawis. Katie Silvy at the time, she grew up in a "picture perfect family" that went to church every Sunday. However, after her parents divorced when Katie was twelve years old, she began a catastrophic slide into sin. As a middle school student, Katie began to steal alcohol from her parent's liquor cabinet and smoke cigarettes and marijuana for the first time. By high school, she was getting drunk every weekend and her marijuana smoking increased to a daily activity. During her senior year of high school, Katie was hanging out with drug dealers and began experimenting with all kinds of drugs including LSD, cocaine, ecstasy, GHB, and prescription pain pills. She would experiment with different combinations of those drugs mixed with marijuana and alcohol. However, since she was excelling in school with honors and AP classes, the adults around her did not think there was much of a problem.

When Katie arrived for college in Gainesville, she decided to attend Santa Fe Community College with aspirations of attending the University of Florida afterward. She continued in her daily addiction of drugs and alcohol while excelling in school. She hung out mostly with guys because guys were "more laid back and didn't let things bother them," and she eventually became a roommate in a household of college men. One day at SFCC she was met by a disciple of Jesus. They began to have great discussions about God and church and Katie shared her philosophies on the subjects. She shared about the many churches she had unsuccessfully tried and how she had now adopted the philosophy that you don't need church to worship God. She now believed that her relationship with God was "personal" and that church was just a business trying to make money. The Christian brother patiently shared scriptures with her and one day invited her to an Easter Sunday service at our church. I met Katie that day at church for the first time, not knowing anything about her past and upbringing. However, I did preach that day about people who only come to church on Christmas and Easter and think that is a relationship with God. She was very convicted as we spoke after service that day; however, that was only the beginning of the battle for her soul. By the time she left service that day, many college disciples had spoken with her and she had exchanged phone numbers with eight different campus women.

As Katie began to study the Bible with disciples, the subject of drug and alcohol use quickly came up. Katie wrestled tirelessly with the Scriptures, struggling to see how marijuana use was a sin since it was not listed explicitly in Scripture (in her opinion). She fought with the sisters over this issue, always leaving convicted but not ready to surrender. One scripture that really helped her was 1 Peter 4:7, which says, "Be clear minded and self-controlled so that you can pray" and also the passage in 1 Thessalonians 5:17, which tells us to "pray continually." After being convicted by the Scriptures, she immediately quit drinking and doing drugs. She moved out of her bad living situation and moved in with spiritual college women. After being baptized, she began to preach the word of God to many college students, helping numerous campus women to become disciples. Katie has been married now to an incredible man named David for ten years and has two beautiful children. Dave and Katie lead a weekly Bible study group in their home, as well as help to lead our Chemical Recovery Group in the church. Within the Chemical Recovery Group, Katie helps to provide spiritual counseling and accountability for women who struggle with alcohol, drug or smoking addiction.

26 students who said, "Here am I. Send me!"

Throughout our first twelve years as a church, we have seen twenty-six college students come through our campus ministry and decide to give up their secular ambitions to serve God in the full-time ministry. To God's glory, we have been able to send out twenty-three of them to other churches to serve as full-time paid staff within campus or teen ministries. Most of them serve throughout the United States, although three of them are currently serving in

Brazil. Here is a list of who they are and where they have gone:

Stuart and Ashley Mains (Los Angeles, CA)

Jake and Kelsey Rock (Los Angeles, CA)

Matt and Simara Blair (St. Louis, MO)

Alex and Melissa Forges (Miami, FL)

Marcus and Amy Overstreet (Jacksonville, and Fort Lauderdale, FL)

Joe Bruno (Baton Rouge, LA; Charlotte, NC; Orlando, FL)

Lauren Scott (Atlanta, GA)

Jon Sherwood (Atlanta, GA; Auburn, AL; Tallahassee, FL)

John and Kay Hoyt (Palm Beach, FL; Santiago, Chile; Brazilia, Brazil)

Amanda Bartoli (Tampa, FL; Norfolk, VA; Charleston, WV)

Chase and Sarah Mackintosh (Cincinnati, OH)

Britney Wilson (Gainesville, FL)

Kyle Eastman (Gainesville, FL)

Tiffany Chacon (Gainesville, FL)

Nilson Ramirez (New York, NY)

Stephen and Roxanne Little (Gwinnett, GA)

Kristi Colson (Brazilia, Brazil)

Joe Clouse (San Diego, CA)

There are so many other young men and women whom I have personally witnessed change their lives completely due to the power of the cross. As the lead evangelist for the Gainesville Christian Church for the past twelve years, I have seen approximately 300 college students and about 100 young single professionals come to faith in Jesus Christ, repent of their sins, and get baptized as disciples of Jesus. It has been incredible and absolutely to the glory of God! I stand in awe at every baptism when the new convert is asked, "What is your good confession?" and he or she responds with conviction by saying, "Jesus is Lord!" These Christians have gone on to make countless sacrifices and live in defiance of the world due to their relationship with God through Jesus Christ. My main question to you is this: How has the cross affected your life?

A great friend of mine whom I had the privilege of mentoring for four years at the University of Florida is Nilson Ramirez. An accomplished writer, he is now twenty-four years old and serves as a campus minister in New York City. He once wrote:

<u>Make up</u> will never <u>make up</u> for what you lose.
When you <u>make up</u> a new you that cares more about your lashes...
than His,
It's the <u>wrong foundation.</u>

As you make up a new you, resolutely decide that your foundation will be the cross of Christ. Don't serve Jesus because of the reward of heaven, the avoidance of hell, or the friendships within the church. While those are fantastic gifts that we receive through Jesus, our motivation must be focused on his sacrifice. When our motivation is deep, there will be nothing in our lives that we are unwilling to give up for our Lord.

As we share our faith with non-Christians, our basic message should be this: "I used to be.... However, today I am.... The reason for my change is the death, burial and resurrection of Jesus Christ." That is how a person lives on the right side of Easter!

Small Group Discussion Questions for Chapter Six

1. The message of the first-century Christians was that Jesus rose from the dead. Is this still the message of Christians today? Is the resurrection of Jesus a big focus in your life?

2. If it was proven tomorrow that Jesus never resurrected from the grave (hypothetically, of course), how would your life change? What would be different about your day tomorrow?

3. If you are a Christian today, how has your life changed? Describe who you used to be, who you are today, and how the resurrection of Jesus played a role in your transformation.

Chapter Seven

—

How Can *I* Change the World?

God: "I hear that a lot—people want to change the world, but don't know how to begin. You want to know how to change the world, son? One act of random kindness at a time."

—Evan Almighty

I hope that by now you have a desire to help change the world. By now you should be asking yourself "What can I do? What can one person do to really change the world?" Here are some suggestions.

How Can I Change the World? Set Your Mind.

According to Colossians 3:2, we need to set our minds "on things above, not on earthly things." The world is relentless in its desire to *train your brain* every day through music, television, Internet, radio, and the like. Therefore, you must be relentless in allowing God to *train your brain* through the Scriptures. By reading your Bible daily, you follow the instructions that God gave to Joshua.

"Be strong and very courageous. Be careful to obey all the law my servant Moses gave you; do not turn from it to the right or to the left, that you may be successful wherever you go. Do not let this Book of the Law depart from

your mouth; *meditate on it day and night,* so that you may be careful to do everything written in it. Then you will be prosperous and successful."
—Joshua 1:7–8, emphasis added

The Israelites were at their best spiritually when they recognized and worshipped God daily. Do you remember in the Old Testament how God would lead the Israelites by a pillar of cloud during the day and a pillar of fire at night? That cloud and fire were *daily reminders* of God's existence. When the cloud moved, the Israelites moved. When the cloud stopped, the people stopped. As soon as they woke up, they saw the pillar and were reminded of the God that they served. It is no wonder that so many different religions throughout history have built altars and erected statues of their gods. They, too, want to be reminded every day that their god exists and is right beside them.

What do you do to remind yourself every day of God's existence? Imagine if God was physically in your bedroom when you woke up and spoke directly to you. How would that change your day? I know it sounds a little crazy, but imagine if God appeared to you at bedside every morning in a pillar of cloud and every night in a pillar of fire as you went to bed. You would feel so much joy every morning as you listened intently to God and he gave you instructions about your day. You could communicate back and forth with him and tell him how much you love him and all that you want to do for him. Then, at the end of the day, you could once again communicate with God about how your day actually went, celebrating the victories and learning from the defeats. This is actually the kind of relationship that God wants to have with us—one of daily intimacy.

Do you realize that Jesus had this kind of daily intimacy with his Father?

Very early in the morning, while it was still dark, Jesus got up, left the house and went off to a solitary place, where he prayed.

—Mark 1:35

If Jesus, even though he was perfect, needed to spend time with his Father each morning, how much more so do you and I?

In today's world, we have many distractions. If you are anything like me, then as soon as you awake your mind is flooded with the numerous things that you need to accomplish that day. For me, my average Tuesday looks like this: staff meeting at 9:00 a.m., discipling time with my campus minister at 10:30 a.m., married brothers luncheon at noon, workout at 1:30 p.m., take my kids to basketball practice and spend time with them at 3:30 p.m., dinner at 6:00 p.m., discipling time with my congregational teacher and his wife at 7:00 p.m., a Bible study with a non-Christian at 8:30 p.m. and go to bed around 11:00 p.m. In between, I need to go to the bank, pay the electric bill, make some follow-up phone calls...you get the point. I assume your day can be just as hectic as mine. In my experience counseling college students, I have discovered one simple truth: If you do not spend time with God before you leave the house in the morning, then you likely will not do it all day.

One of the ways that I remind myself of God's presence is that, as soon as I roll out of bed and my feet touch the floor, I frequently drop to my hands and knees to pray. Even though I am still a bit groggy, I take the time to recognize my Lord and to praise his name before I do anything else in my day. This is generally a shorter prayer time as I know the bulk of my prayer time will happen later on. However, I do it because God deserves it and I want to remind myself that Jesus is Lord of every second of my day.

How Can I Change the World? One Person at a Time.

Throughout history, no one wanted to change the world more than Jesus Christ! How did he attempt to do it? He could have become an important political figure (after all, the world has never heard from a better speaker) or he could have become a famous physician (imagine Jesus developing a cure for AIDS hundreds of years before the virus even arrived). However, that is not what he did. No, Jesus attempted to change the world one person at a time. While Jesus spoke regularly to large crowds, he also spoke often to individuals about their relationship with his Father. Think about all the one-on-one encounters with Jesus that the Bible records: Zacchaeus (Luke 19), the woman at the well (John 4), the rich young man (Mark 10) and the conversion of Saul (Acts 9), just to name a few. Even after Jesus' ascension to heaven, there were only about 120 Christians standing with Peter (Acts 1:15). Jesus was not interested in a mass conversion movement that would only last for a single generation. Instead, he wanted to focus his efforts on finding the few who would turn the world upside down.

What if, over the next twelve months, you focused on converting one person? That's right—just one person. However, in converting this one person, you made it your goal to pour yourself into them in a Colossians 1:28–29 sort of way.

> We proclaim him, admonishing and teaching everyone with all wisdom, so that we may present everyone perfect in Christ. To this end I labor, struggling with all his energy, which so powerfully works in me.
>
> —Colossians 1:28–29

According to this passage, you would need to labor (work vigorously) in order to help this person become perfect in Christ. You would need to struggle (in prayer and in action) in order to train them to be like Jesus. That means that, after they are baptized, you would ensure that many follow-up Bible studies are done. Additionally, you would periodically have quiet times together, go out sharing your faith together, get into Bible studies with non-Christians together, eat some meals together, go to the movies together, and have discipling times together. Not only that, but you would make sure that they are devoted to the body by helping them to attend Sunday services, midweek services and small group Bible studies. On top of all that, you will need to encourage them to go on great dates with other Christians (you may even need to set this up at first). Helping someone to walk with Jesus is a wonderful challenge. Are you up for it?

Now imagine if every Christian in your campus or singles or teen ministry took on this challenge? What if each Christian focused, over the next twelve months, on converting one person and lovingly training them to walk with Jesus? What would your ministry look like after twelve months?

In the spring of 2000, I got to meet an incredible young man named Marcus Overstreet. Marcus was getting his masters degree from the University of Florida in sports management and was cohosting a morning radio talk show about Gator sports. I first met him when his sister, Lavogna Drabot, called me from North Carolina and told me about her brother at UF. She asked if I would call him, because he might be open to studying the Bible. Even though Marcus blew me off on the phone call, he came to church a few months later and we finally met face to face. From that moment on, we became best friends. We began to meet together at restaurants and in my home to study the Bible, as well as meeting up at the gym to work out or going to the UF football stadium to run the steps. I called various brothers like Greg Grooms or Joe Bruno or John Hoyt to encourage them to talk with Marcus, as I knew that he would need a village of spiritual friends in his life. After a couple of weeks, Marcus was baptized into Christ! We soon began to have follow-up studies where I (or one of the brothers) would show Marcus a plethora of scriptures about walking with God and general spiritual growth. We shared our faith together and got into many Bible studies with non-Christians together. I encouraged him to go on many dates with Christian women and would listen to the stories afterward. Additionally, I would save him a seat at church or make sure that someone else was doing the same. Even when his father passed away, I was right there to cry with him. We laughed together, dreamed together, prayed together. He simply became a part of my family. Eventually, Marcus fell in love with a Christian woman named Amy and I had the privilege of serving as his best man in the wedding.

One of the most difficult decisions I ever had to make was when a need came up in another church and they needed a strong campus minister. I recommended Marcus for the job and, in 2003, he moved to Jacksonville, Florida. Today Marcus serves as a Regional Church Leader within the South Florida Church of Christ. He now has three children and in November 2011 was appointed as an evangelist. I was sitting in the second row of the service that day holding his mother's hand and crying as he was appointed. My relationship with Marcus has changed over the years from big brother/little brother to a peer relationship. He is now preaching the word of God each week to hundreds of people and helping many people grow in their relationship with God. You never know; by converting one person, you just might end up helping hundreds.

Even if the person you help to convert doesn't go into the full-time ministry, they will still live a lifetime of devotion to God and end up helping hundreds of people. I do not want you to feel like you have to reach the masses in order to change the world. You don't. You just need to reach one person each year and train them to be a true follower of Jesus.

How Can I Change the World? Be Salty.

Consider the words of Jesus:

> "You are the salt of the earth. But if the salt loses its saltiness, how can it be made salty again? It is no longer good for anything, except to be thrown out and trampled by men."

—Matthew 5:13

Who is Jesus talking to when he says, "You are the salt of the earth"? The Christians! That's you. That's me. In God's eyes, we are viewed as salt. What does that mean? Well, the purpose of salt is for preserving and flavoring. That means that, as Christians, we are the vessels that God uses to preserve the life of Christ in the earth. As one commentary says, "Christians are to the human race what salt is to food: the element which preserves it from corruption and gives savor and relish."[11] How cool is that? You and I are chosen to preserve the message of Jesus so that it does not grow stale in the eyes of the world. Additionally, you and I are chosen to be the flavor/ the impact/the conviction of this world! Oh, yeah!

Have you ever eaten some McDonald's french fries? While they are unhealthy, they taste oh, so good! Now imagine eating those same french fries with no salt on them. Would you still like to eat them? No way! It is the salt that makes them taste so good! It is the same way with potato chips and popcorn. They taste great with salt but have virtually no flavor without salt. My point is this: Without the Christians, this world is like tasteless french fries! Without you and me, this world is boring and the message of Jesus will become corrupted! However, if we lose our saltiness (lose our impact), we are no longer good for anything. Therefore, we must make a difference in this world!

Consider the words of Paul:

> Let your conversation be always full of grace, *seasoned with salt*, so that you may know how to answer everyone.
>
> —Colossians 4:6, emphasis added

According to this passage, our conversations must always contain two things: grace and salt. What does it mean for your conversation to be "full of grace" and "seasoned with salt"? Our grace comes from the fact that everyone is a sinner and falls short of the glory of God (Romans 3:23–24). Our saltiness comes from the convictions we have gained through the Bible. Therefore, when you speak to Christians and non-Christians alike, they should feel like you care and have compassion while also understanding that you will hold yourself and others to the standards of the Bible.

Are you considered a salty person? Do people in your church or your household think of you as salty? What if I was speaking to your ministry and I asked them, "Who is the saltiest person in this group?" Would anyone say your name? While there is certainly a time to talk about sports, movies, music, hobbies and politics, a salty person is more interested in discussing items that relate to a person's walk with God. For example, what do you talk about immediately after church? Do you discuss your upcoming lunch location? Perhaps the big game that just happened? Or do you find a friend and ask, "What did you get out of that sermon today?" or "What are you currently studying in the Bible?" or "What can I pray about for you?" I want to encourage you to be salty! Often, our tendency is to divert conversations into safe areas that have no lasting spiritual effects. You are called to be different! You are called to be salty!

There have been many times when I have had to be salty with Christians and non-Christians in my life. Have you ever seen someone who is consistently late for church or small group discussions? Have you ever seen someone who is consistently lazy about getting a job or completing his classes? Have you ever been out with someone who tends to have one too many alcoholic drinks? Have you ever thought to yourself, "That dating couple seems to spend a lot of alone time together. I wonder how their purity is going?" What do you do when you are in these types of situations? One time I was developing a new friendship with a neighbor of mine in Miami and we were heading off to play some basketball. As we were driving to the courts, he was continually cursing in our conversation. Almost every sentence had a curse word. He wasn't angry; it just came out as he spoke. Since our friendship was only about a week old, I knew that I needed to be delicate with my approach. However, I just couldn't ignore his foul language. "Why do you curse so much?" I asked him. "Do you think that it will make people like you more?" He was shocked at my words. He looked at me and said, "I don't know. No one has ever asked me that question before. I really have no reason for it." As we talked more about it, he eventually said, "I think I would like to try to quit cursing. Will you help me?"

Are you willing to *hunt to confront?* Are you willing to be a *guardian of the church*?

I hope that you love God and his people enough to initiate the difficult conversations when you see sin in the camp. Even if you are a young Christian, please don't let that stop you! You signed up to follow Jesus just like the rest of us. Remember that Colossians 4:6 was not written to older Christians only; it was written to all Christians! We are all charged with the task of being salty.

How Can I Change the World? Live Cheap and Donate.

All they asked was that we should continue to remember the poor, the very thing I was eager to do.

—Galatians 2:10

We generally do not like the word "cheap." However, the idea here is to live below your means, make calculated sacrifices within your living expenses, and then give the money that you would have otherwise spent on yourself to the poor or to charities that serve the poor. It is a pretty simple concept, but one that strikes at the heart of our worldliness and materialism.

It is amazing how rich we are as Americans compared to other parts of the world. We get frustrated when our Internet does not work fast enough or if our "fast food" is too slow in coming out to the table. However, in many other parts of the world, people have no quality shelter, little food to eat, or no clean water to drink. If you have never visited a third world country, I would highly recommend it. It just might change your life. It will certainly make you more grateful for the material blessings that you have.

Often, we think that we need to wait until we get older and have a big job before we can really be sacrificial and give financially. We think that there is not much we can really do while we are in college or working as a young professional. Therefore, why try? That is exactly how Satan wants you to think. You must understand:

The habits you establish as a young adult are the habits you will carry throughout life!

If you eat healthy now, you will most likely eat healthy all your life. If exercise is important to you now, you will most likely exercise all your life. The same is true with donating money and serving the poor. Even if your sacrifice is small in comparison to someone else's sacrifice, it will still be a big deal to you and an even bigger deal to God. The Bible has much to say about taking care of the poor and overcoming our own love for money.

I teach my two children about money by saying this: "Money is useful for three things: spending, saving and giving away." Every time they received their allowance as small children, they would divide it up into three envelopes: one for spending, one for saving and one for giving away. It was always comical to Kim and me as Corey would put the majority of his money into the "savings" or "giving away" envelope while Taylor would put almost all of her money into the "spending" or "giving away" envelope. Basically, Corey did not like to spend his money and Taylor did not like to save her money. It showed insight into their personalities and priorities. How would you divide up your money?

A recent UF graduate from our campus ministry, David Berndt, went on a mission trip to Asunción, Paraguay in 2011 and was stunned at how other human beings live: no clean water, children without shoes, and large families sharing a one-bedroom "house" with only one bed! From that trip, God put on his heart the idea to start a "Live Cheap" movement (www.livecheap.org) where he speaks to others, notably college students, about making regular sacrifices in their own lifestyle so that they can give money to the poor. He encourages students to use cheaper cell phones that do not include Web access, take public transportation rather than own a car, or simply shop for clothing at thrift stores. Obviously, there are many ways that we can make daily lifestyle sacrifices (how much did that Starbucks coffee cost?) on items that may simply be a luxury in our lives. The idea is then to take your "saved money" by living cheap and donate it to a charity or a nonprofit organization. This is a great example of how one Christian can help change the world.

How Can I Change the World? Mentor a Child.

> People were bringing little children to Jesus to have him touch them, but the disciples rebuked them. When Jesus saw this, he was indignant. He said to them, "Let the little children come to me."
>
> —Mark 10:13–14

Jesus loved to be around the children. Obviously some of the disciples did not think that children were a worthy use of the Lord's time, but Jesus rebuked them for such thoughts. Do you enjoy being around elementary school children or middle school kids? Do you even know any of the names of the kids at church?

When I first got married, I told Kim that I did not want to have kids. I honestly felt that children simply got in the way of having fun or accomplishing my dreams. However, when I became a Christian at the age of twenty-four, I began to change my mind. I saw incredible dads in the church along with obedient, loving children. My mind really changed when I met a two-year-old named T.J. Deam. He was the son of Doug and Ann Deam, some good friends of ours, and T.J.

would run and jump into my arms after every church service. He would call me "Twoy." I would look forward to seeing him at every service and would carry him around in the fellowship.

I think too many college students, especially the young men, do not look at the children and youth of the church in a spiritual way. Many of the college students do not understand what a role model they can be and how such a little amount of effort can mean so much to a child. When you were a kid, did you have anyone from the age of eighteen to thirty who served as a role model for you? If so, then you know how valuable their influence was in your life. It only took a little bit of their time for you to feel really special. If you did not have such a person, imagine how your childhood may have been different if you did. Imagine the mistakes you may have avoided and the insecurities you may have overcome if someone would have invested in you (besides your parents).

I am very grateful for the college students at the Gainesville Christian Church who serve as mentors for our youth. In our church, we have a mentoring program where everyone in our high school ministry (grades 9 through 12) and everyone in our middle school ministry (grades 5 through 8) gets a college student to serve as a mentor. Sometimes, even the children younger than fifth grade will have a mentor. Basically, we ask the college mentor to spend time with the child once or twice every month by going out for ice cream, playing video games, or doing whatever it takes to connect on their level. We also ask the mentor to have an age-appropriate spiritual conversation at some point during their time together. This has been an amazing success as many of our college students have served in this way and impacted dozens of young people. Often, the college student even gets pulled in to the family and receives many great benefits for themselves like food, advice and love (did I mention food?).

As a parent, I am extremely grateful when anyone takes a genuine interest in my child. There is probably not a better way to show your love for me than loving up on my children. It hits my heart tremendously. I am eternally grateful for the mentors in my children's lives. Over the last couple of years, John Wilson and Joe Clouse have poured themselves into my eleven-year-old son, Corey. At first, it was John who would come over to the house and hang out with my son. When John was no longer able to mentor Corey, Joe stepped in. Joe picks up Corey every other Sunday morning and takes him out for breakfast before church. Corey always brings his Bible and they read together for a while. Please allow me to tell you a "Corey story": As I am writing this portion of the book on March 12, 2012, Kim and I got up this morning to get the kids ready for school as we always do. Kim went into Corey's room to find him sitting on the floor reading his Bible (he was studying Acts 5). When Kim asked him what he was doing, Corey said that Joe had encouraged him to read his Bible and pray before school every day this week. How cool is that? While I have encouraged him to do that many times before, sometimes it is the words of a mentor that make all the difference.

While Corey's personality is to have a few close friends, Taylor, my nine-year-old daughter, enjoys having a plethora of friends. Thus, she has had many more mentors over the last few years. I am really grateful for Tiffany Chacon, Tiffany Hoffman, Brittney Jennaford, Alie Trainor, Jennifer Fix, Britney Wilson, Courtney Liffrig, and Alex Johnson. These girls have each taken Taylor out for smoothies or ice cream, simply serving as a big sister for her. Taylor has even gone over to a few of their houses for spend-the-night parties (Taylor's favorite way to connect). Often times these mentors will come over for dinner at my house and then come with us to one of Taylor's basketball games or other events. They have become a part of our family!

What can you do as an individual to change the world? Mentor a child. Pray and get advice about who you can invest some of your time into. It is of vital importance that we pass on the torch to the next generation!

How Can I Change the World? Be a Light Within Your Family.

In Matthew 10:37, Jesus said, "Anyone who loves his father or mother more than me is not worthy of me; anyone who loves his son or daughter more than me is not worthy of me; and anyone who does not take his cross and follow me is not worthy of me."

Jesus' point is that our family cannot come before him! Ever! In order to be considered by Jesus to be a follower, we must be willing to obey his commands, even if it goes against our parents' or our children's desires. This can be a difficult teaching. Certainly, the Bible teaches that we need to honor our father and mother (Ephesians 6:2). I have two children and I want them to obey the things that I tell them (Colossians 3:20). However, if I begin to teach them things that are against God's word, they have a biblical mandate to obey God's word over mine. After all, I will not be standing beside them on Judgment Day. The Bible teaches that we will all stand alone before God and give an account of our lives (Hebrews 4:13). Unfortunately, I have seen too many college students back away from their commitment to Jesus because their parents felt that they were becoming "too committed" to studying the Bible, going to church or helping others. In some cases, I have seen college students repent of their drug use, failure in school and overall wild lifestyle, only to be brought down by parents who did not approve of their new faith in Jesus. Other times, I have seen college students stand firm in their faith, not back down to family persecution, and eventually win over their family to Jesus. It always comes back to the question: Is Jesus really your Lord?

When Kim and I were baptized as disciples on July 14, 1996, my family gave me a hard time. My mom and older brother Jason both strongly disapproved of my newfound biblical convictions and of my decision to get baptized. However, I compounded the problem by trying to preach my new convictions to my family—don't ever do that! In my zeal, I wanted to show them the scriptures that had helped me to change my life, hoping that they would have the same effect on my family. However, as Proverbs 19:2 says, "It is not good to have zeal without knowledge, nor to be hasty and miss the way." I failed to realize that my actions could cause me to appear self-righteous and cause my family to feel insecure or even competitive. I was not giving them the same opportunity that I had received, which was to see the gospel in action through the disciples and then to be taught the Scriptures by friends in a loving environment. Even though my intentions were good, I now know that I should have behaved differently and I apologized for my actions. After realizing my error, I learned a huge lesson:

The key to reaching out to your family is to share about you, not about them.

As Jesus was getting into the boat, the man who had been demon-possessed begged to go with him. Jesus did not let him, but said "Go home to your family and tell them how much the Lord has done for you, and how he has had mercy on you."

—Mark 5:18–19

What do you notice in Jesus' instructions to the new convert about how to deal with his family? He said to "tell them how much the Lord has done for you." Do you see it? Jesus wants us to share the gospel with our families, but he wants us to do it the right way.

Instead of talking about what is deficient in their lives, share the joy of what is happening in *your* life. Share the good news about what you are learning in your Bible studies or how you are helping to make disciples. Let your family see the difference in your life when you go home by doing the dishes or asking to help around the house. Don't be the same lazy or selfish person that you may have been before. Let Jesus shine through your actions. It is good to tell your family how different you are now because of God; it is even better to show them.

For the next few years after our conversion, Kim and I simply shared with our families the good news about what God was doing in our lives. God blessed our repentance, perseverance and prayer as Kim's mother, Jean Brown, studied the Bible, said, "Jesus is Lord" and was baptized as a true disciple in 1998! Today, she is a strong Christian woman in the Gainesville Christian Church who counsels many other women. Then in 1999, my only brother, Jason Criss, said, "Jesus is Lord" and became a Christian! I am eternally grateful for brothers like Kenton Kennedy, Mike Hodges, and Hilton Soto, who studied the Bible with Jason and allowed me to simply be the sounding board for my brother after each study. He is now married to a great Christian woman named Rachel, has two beautiful sons named Brian and Brandon, and is the deacon of ushers at GCC. Then in 2003, Kim's father, Dawson Brown, began to study the Bible with some of the older men in the church and he was baptized as well! Today, he is a strong disciple at GCC and serves on our financial count team. Then in 2006, Kim's grandmother, Ennis Woodley, at the age of 86, became too old to live alone in Jacksonville any longer. She moved to Gainesville to live with Kim's parents after having attended a different denomination for the past 70 years of her life. She was moved in her heart by the zeal that she saw in the church and after attending for six months, she approached me and said, "I have never seen a group of college students who love God so much. It is really inspiring! Troy, I would like to be a member of your church but I was baptized as a young girl and it took! So what do we need to do?" I said, "Well, grandma, I think you need to study the Bible with the older ladies and make sure that we all have the same convictions about Jesus." Grandma said, "OK, but I would like to have you in all of my Bible studies." I agreed to her request. Thus, I was in every one of her studies (ever done a sin study with your grandma before?) as we looked at many scriptures together for about one month. After that time, she realized that she needed to repent of her sins, confess "Jesus is Lord" and get baptized for the forgiveness of her sins. It was glorious! Grandma is now ninety-one years old and is a faithful member of our congregation! Sometimes it is hard to break through family traditions, but I believe that if you will stay true to your convictions and love your families deeply, then God will bless your perseverance and bring peace to your family.

The key is to serve our families and be a light to them. Even if they never change their views about God or become Christians, God is still pleased and glorified by your actions.

How Can I Change the World? Never Quit!

> Lance Armstrong: "I think you better hurry up or you're gonna be late (for the finals)."
>
> Peter LeFleur: "Actually, I decided to quit, Lance."

Lance Armstrong: "Quit?! You know once I was thinking about quitting, when I was diagnosed with brain, lung and testicular cancer, all at the same time. But with the love and support of my friends and family I got back on the bike and I won the Tour de France five times in a row. But I'm sure you have a good reason to quit. (pause) So what are you dying from that's keeping you from the finals?"

Peter LeFleur: "Right now, it feels a little bit like...shame."

Lance Armstrong: "Well, I guess if a person never quit when the going got tough, they wouldn't have anything to regret for the rest of their life. (pause) Well, good luck to you, Peter. I'm sure this decision won't haunt you forever."

—*Dodgeball*

Quitting is the worst thing you can ever do as a Christian. I will say that again: Quitting is the worst thing you can ever do as a Christian. Will we sin? Of course. Will we sin to the point of embarrassment? Probably. However, as long as we continually get back up again and turn back to Jesus in repentance, he will forgive us.

Let us not become weary in doing good, for at the proper time we will reap a harvest if we do not give up.

—Galatians 6:9

But we are not of those who shrink back and are destroyed, but of those who believe and are saved.

—Hebrews 10:39

Satan wants you to quit. Satan wants you to get tired of doing the right things: sharing your faith, denying yourself of sin, spending time and money in spiritual ways. Satan wants you to shrink back in your faith and not confess your struggles to other Christians. Remember Chapter 3? Satan is your enemy and is scheming about how to take you out. You must learn to persevere through trials, even fatigue. Remember Chapter 6? If your eyes are fixed on the cross, you will be able to fight through your trials.

> Consider him who endured such opposition from sinful men, so that you will not grow weary and lose heart.
>
> In your struggle against sin, you have not yet resisted to the point of shedding your blood.
>
> —Hebrews 12:3–4

Remember: the Christian life is a marathon, not a sprint. It doesn't do much good for you to start out your Christian life with a lot of zeal, only to fall by the wayside at the end. If you ever begin to lose heart for the gospel, simply remember Jesus. The thought of his death and the joy of his resurrection will continually inspire you to get back on the narrow road.

How Can I Change the World?

There are some things that you as an individual can do to change the world—set your mind daily, convert one person at a time, be salty, live cheap and donate, mentor a child, be a light within your family, and never give up. However, there are some atrocities in this world that can only be changed by the Holy Spirit working through a large group of Christians. This is what we will discuss in the next chapter.

Small Group Discussion Questions for Chapter Seven

1. How important do you believe it is to study God's word every day? How do you see the world attempting to train your brain every day?

2. Have you ever helped convert someone to Jesus and then poured months into helping to train them in the Lord? Talk about your experience. How would it change your life if you focused on converting one person each year with the intention of investing in that person and training them to be like Jesus?

3. What do you think it means to "let your conversation be always full of grace, seasoned with salt"? Are you a salty person? Would others say that you are? In what ways should you be saltier?

4. How do you feel about the words "live cheap and donate"? In what areas could a person make calculated sacrifices and then donate that money to charity? Do you think that this would please God?

5. Have you ever mentored a child before? If yes, describe the experience. Did you ever have a mentor when you were a child? If yes, describe the experience. How might your adolescent struggles have been different if you had a mentor who invested in you?

6. Is your family supportive of your convictions about Jesus and church? How can you do a better job of serving your family and being a light in your home?

7. Why do you think some people become Christians and then later quit? How can you stay strong in the faith?

Chapter Eight

—

How Can *We* Change the World?

Agent Morales: "As one stick may break, a bundle is strong."
—Act of Valor

Airport clerk: "Sir, you can't go in there!"
Harry: "It's OK, I'm a limo driver!"

—Dumb and Dumber

Sometimes, we just need crazy faith! We just need to believe that we can do incredible things through God, even if it seems unlikely to others. In Chapter 7, we talked about some ways that we can help change the world as individuals. In this chapter, I would like for us to dream about what God could do if all the Christians worked together. There are some problems in this world that are simply too large to change by ourselves. However, when the Christians are all focused in one direction, there is a strength that cannot be defeated. At our Friday night campus devotional last week, I asked our 100-member Campus Ministry about this subject. I asked them about the things that they believe can change in this world if we all worked together. Basically, I wanted to know what the college students were passionate about and what they wanted to see change in our society. (I had put the same question to our Professionals Ministry a few weeks earlier.) Some of the ideas that we are about to discuss have come from those two groups.

Please allow me to share with you some *major problems* in our world today and let's discuss the *role of the Christians* in helping to change them.

Championing Abstinence Before Marriage

Cameron Diaz: "Don't you know that when you sleep with someone, your body makes a promise whether you do or not?"

—*Vanilla Sky*

According to www.thefreedictionary.com, the definition of abstinence is "the act or practice of refraining from indulging an appetite or desire, especially for alcoholic drink or sexual intercourse." For anyone who has said, "Jesus is Lord" and continues to live as a true disciple, the idea of abstinence before marriage is something that you have embraced. However, many Americans have not made that decision yet. Please allow me to give you some statistics from a website on sex before marriage.

According to webmd.com and the Guttmacher Institute, one-fourth of all fifteen-year-olds in the U.S. have had sexual intercourse at least once, and more than half of all seventeen-year-olds are sexually active. The risks are even more startling: A sexually active teenage girl who has sex without contraception has a 90% chance of becoming pregnant within a year. Not only that, but in a single act of sexual intercourse with an infected male partner, a female teenager has a 30% risk of contracting genital herpes, a 50% chance of contracting gonorrhea, and a 1 in 100 chance of acquiring HIV. The Medical Institute for Sexual Health estimates that 20% of all Americans age twelve and older are currently infected with genital herpes.

According to The Centers for Disease Control and Prevention, the U.S. has the highest teenage pregnancy rate of all developed countries *in the world!* About one million teenagers become pregnant each year; 95% of those pregnancies are unintended, and almost one-third end in abortions.

According to the National Center on Addiction and Substance Abuse at Columbia University, 88% of fifteen-to twenty-four-year-olds say that people their age drink or use drugs before having sex at least "sometimes"—50% say this happens "a lot." Additionally, when it comes to date rape among college students, alcohol used by the victim, perpetrator, or both, has been implicated in 46 to 75% of the incidents.

According to the A.C. Green Youth Foundation, among sexually active teens, eight out of ten girls and six out of ten boys say that they wish they had waited to have sex.[12]

I realize that I just gave you a lot of numbers, but remember we are not just dealing with numbers...we are dealing with young people. We are talking about the lives of high school students, college students and young professionals. I want you to also realize that the consequences of sex can be even more painful than pregnancy or sexually transmitted diseases. Sex before marriage can ruin your heart. It can cause you to struggle with trust issues for the rest of your life. When you have sex with someone, especially for a woman, you give part of yourself to that person, and it can be very difficult to ever get over the failed relationship. It can cause you to doubt people's motives in future relationships. It can ruin your dreams and ruin your future. Abstinence is the only way to ensure 100% protection from all of these consequences.

Satan has created a lie. Satan has caused so many young women to believe that young men won't like them unless they are sexual with them, that they won't be accepted unless they "give them what they want." That is simply not true. Satan has caused many young men to believe that they will be viewed as "weird" if they do not pursue women for sex or talk "a big game" as if this is what they are all about. Once again, this is a lie from Satan. Do not believe it.

Did you know that Shippensburg University in Pennsylvania now has vending machines on its campus where students can buy the "morning-after" pill? That's right, vending machines! On that campus, college students can slip $25 into the vending machine and receive a pill that can prevent pregnancy if taken soon after sexual intercourse. Federal law makes the pill available without a prescription to anyone seventeen or older and, since the school records showed that all current students were that age or older, the school decided to sell the product on campus.[13] How crazy is that?! In my opinion, this encourages students to be more sexually active. When your vending machine options are chewing gum, a Snickers bar or the "morning-after" pill, doesn't that make sex seem casual? This may not be on your campus today, but it is an indicator of where our world is heading.

I believe that the Christian nation of young people needs to stand up loudly on this issue! Any high school student, college student or young professional who is a follower of Jesus needs to not only practice abstinence before marriage, but they need to be vocal about it! When you have opportunity, talk about it—in private among friends and in public among larger groups. Do not be ashamed! You have made the right choice—there is no question about that! However, you must help others to understand that there is another way to live. And when they ask you why you abstain from sex, look them directly in the eyes and say "Jesus."

> But among you there must not be even a hint of sexual immorality, or of any kind of impurity, or of greed, because these are improper for God's holy people.... For of this you can be sure: No immoral, impure, or greedy person—such a man is an idolater—has any inheritance in the kingdom of Christ and of God.
>
> —Ephesians 5:3, 5

> Treat younger men as brothers, older women as mothers, and younger women as sisters, *with absolute purity.*
>
> —1 Timothy 5:2, emphasis added

We have a strong Christian woman in our Gainesville campus ministry named Tiffany Chacon. When Tiffany was a freshman at the University of Florida, she was enrolled in a public speaking class where she was required to stand up in front of her fifty classmates and give a persuasive speech on any subject she wanted. While students chose to speak on many different subjects (one girl spoke about why you should go to Key West, Florida for spring break and how to pick up men in the bars), Tiffany spoke on abstinence before marriage. As an eighteen-year-old, she stood confidently before her peers and told them all the reasons for why she has never had sex and makes a daily choice to remain abstinent. She spoke about sexually transmitted diseases and unwanted pregnancies. She read various passages from the Bible and talked about God's will for her life. Tiffany spoke about her relationship with her current boyfriend, Tyler (today Tyler and Tiffany are married), and how abstinence had deepened their relationship and allowed her to trust him more. She was able to communicate the joys of being loved for all the right reasons and not the wrong ones. Before her speech began, Tiffany had to choose for someone in her life to introduce her. Who introduced her that day? Tyler. As Tiffany bravely spoke about a subject that certainly would not be embraced by all her peers, Tyler was right there supporting her. Can you imagine how God must have felt that day? He must have been so pleased to see his children not only living right, but also standing up for him.

In Luke 9:26, Jesus says, "If anyone is ashamed of me and my words, the Son of Man will be ashamed of him when he comes in his glory and in the glory of the Father and of the holy angels." We need more high school students, college students and young professionals to stand up for God's word on this issue! If you have made the decision to be abstinent before marriage, then I want to commend you. You have definitely made the right choice! However, you cannot stop there. There are so many young people who are buying into the lie that sex before marriage is necessary in order to be accepted and that "everyone is doing it." So many people need you (and God needs you) to speak the truth from God's word and from your heart about this issue. Sex before marriage is *a major worldwide problem* and, if the Christians will rise up and speak out on this issue, then God will use us to change the world on the subject!

Overcoming the Racial Divide Within Our Country

The United States is still a segregated country. While we have come a long way in the past fifty years, we are still divided by race. Even though the government began integrating our schools in the

1960s following the Brown v. Board of Education decision, they still cannot make different races live in the same neighborhoods or attend the same churches.

Let's be brutally honest: Sunday is the most segregated day of the week in the U.S. Blacks, whites, Latinos, Chinese, and other races may go to school together Monday through Friday and even compete in the same sports leagues on Saturday, but we typically do not worship God together on Sunday. For some churches, the only black color found inside the building is on the seat cushions. Similarly, for other churches, the only white color found inside the building is on the choir robes. Segregation is not right and it does not please the Lord.

> Then Jesus came to them and said, "All authority in heaven and on earth has been given to me. Therefore go and *make disciples of all nations,* baptizing them in the name of the Father and of the Son and of the Holy Spirit, and teaching them to obey everything I have commanded you. And surely I am with you always, to the very end of the age."
>
> —Matthew 28:18–20, emphasis added

Jesus' final teaching to his disciples was very simple: Go and make disciples of all nations! Don't just reach out to one or two nations, but try to convert them all. Furthermore, Jesus instructs that, once we make someone a disciple, we must then "teach them to obey everything" that Jesus previously instructed. Thus, we must help the new converts to go and make disciples of all nations! Do you see it? Jesus built his plan for integration directly into the Great Commission!

So how did the first-century church do with integration? As Paul began to bring the gospel to different areas of the world (see the book of Acts), many different types of people began to believe in Jesus, repent of their sins and get baptized. It was incredible! However, the church had to wrestle with equality within the church, especially among people who had such a different upbringing or history than their own.

> You are all sons of God through faith in Christ Jesus, for all of you who were baptized into Christ have clothed yourselves with Christ. There is neither Jew nor Greek, slave nor free, male nor female, for you are all *one in Christ Jesus.*
>
> —Galatians 3:26–28, emphasis added

> Here there is no Greek or Jew, circumcised or uncircumcised, barbarian, Scythian, slave or free, but *Christ is all*, and is in all.
>
> Therefore, as God's chosen people, holy and dearly loved, clothe yourselves with compassion, kindness, humility, gentleness and patience.
>
> —Colossians 3:11–12, emphasis added

You may be familiar with the difference between a Greek and a Jew or what it means to be circumcised or uncircumcised. But what do you know about a barbarian or a Scythian? A barbarian was someone who did not speak Greek and was generally thought to be uncivilized. The Scythians were notorious for their savagery and brutality. They were a feared group that drank the blood of the men they killed in battle and were considered by others as little better than wild beasts. Crazy, huh? The point is that they were *extremely different* from a Greek or a Jew. The Greeks, Jews, barbarians and Scythians all came from different backgrounds and cultures. However, Colossians 3:11–12 teaches us that Jesus transcends all racial barriers and unites people from all cultures, races and nations.

Such distinctions between people are no longer significant. Jesus Christ is the only thing that matters!

When Kim and I began the Gainesville Christian Church in 1999, we were determined that it would be an interracial congregation. I am not talking about having one or two people of a different race or even a few different races lightly sprinkled throughout the congregation. On the contrary, we fervently prayed that this church would accurately represent the demographics of our city. As God always does, he has answered our prayers! I can honestly say that GCC has members from dozens of nations and accurately represents the demographics of Gainesville. We are truly an integrated congregation. However, there is still a lot of work to be done. I am not sure if you ever truly "arrive" in this area. It is a daily battle to make sure that everyone "feels" equal in the church and that no favoritism is shown. I work hard to make sure that different races are represented in the podium, within our eldership, on our staff and within the lay leadership. I work extensively with our music leaders to make sure that we are singing songs that don't just appeal to one race but songs that appeal to a spectrum of different races. The singing and worship is so important within the church and so many people have opinions about it. However, it can also be quite divisive if it is not done properly and with careful thought. When I preach, I constantly remind the congregation that we are building a church "of all nations" and thus you must relinquish your desire for the church to only sing songs that match the way you were raised. Building a church of many races isn't easy but it is one of the most joyful parts of what I do. I can only imagine how much glory it must bring to the Lord.

As disciples of Jesus, we need to help bring about change in the area of segregation and discrimination! I truly believe that the younger people, those from the ages of sixteen to thirty-five years old, have the power to transcend our country into a racially unified community. Unfortunately, the truth of the matter is that some of our parents and grandparents have been hurt in the past by racial division and might possibly be set in their ways. However, young people have an opportunity to do something that our parents and grandparents have only dreamed about. We have a long way to go. Racial inequality has been a major problem in the U.S. for a long time and it is going to take a lot of effort to fix it. Are you willing? Are you willing to be best friends with people who have a different skin color than yours? Are you willing to obey Colossians 3:12 and "clothe" yourself with "compassion, kindness, humility, gentleness and patience" as you reach out to people who had a different upbringing than you?

Some of my best friends are men with a different skin color than mine. Last year, I took four other men with me and flew out to Crested Butte, Colorado for a retreat. I went with Oliver Rhoden (a black man), Greg Grooms (a white man), Dave Indarawis (an Egyptian man), and Kenton Kennedy (a Jamaican man). We got quite a few looks from people in the airport. These are some of my best friends. Back in Gainesville, I have two twenty-year-old black men, Dre Orr and Trell Ellerbe, who come over to my house every week for dinner and come with my family to many of our family events. They are big brothers to my children and they refer to Kim and me as "Mom and Dad." I have many white friends as well. My point is that I choose my friends based on character, not color. Is there any racism in your heart? What do your closest friends look like? Do they look just like you? If so, then perhaps you need to repent.

On August 28, 2013, our nation will celebrate the fiftieth

anniversary of the most famous speech ever given about racial equality: "I Have a Dream" by Dr. Martin Luther King. In his speech, Dr. King said, "I have a dream that my four children will one day live in a nation where they will not be judged by the color of their skin but by the content of their character." While we have made many strides, we still have a long way to go. What I want to know is this: Will you be part of the solution? Will you allow people who look different from you to be your roommates in college, your partners in business or your guests for dinner? Will you vow to never judge a person by the color of their skin but only by the content of their character? Will you work hard and pray harder for God to bring about change in the area of segregation and discrimination? I am convinced that the high school students, college students and young professionals *are the key* to unlocking the racial divide in our country and helping to change the world.

Reestablishing the Importance of the Family Unit

Do you remember the popular TV shows of the 1970s and 1980s? People loved TV shows like *The Brady Bunch, Family Ties, The Partridge Family, Family Matters, The Fresh Prince of Bel Air, Home Improvement, Little House on the Prairie* and *The Cosby Show.* These shows depicted the moral values of our country at that time. People wanted television where the father and mother were happily married in the home and raising children. People found it interesting to see family dynamics where the parents had to struggle to work out real issues within their marriage or humorously contend with disagreements with their children.

However, today's television is much different. Today, some of the most popular sitcoms on TV are *How I Met Your Mother, Rules of Engagement* and *Two and Half Men,* where the leading man is single, continually drunk, and in a different sexual relationship every show. For some reason, people seem to envy or look up to the kind of character who is rich, good-looking, witty, driven by sex, and only concerned about himself. People seem to prefer a leading man who has no respect for women and continually puts down the "family" that exists around him. Aren't you amazed at how much our entertainment preferences have changed over one generation? If we continue this trend, what kind of TV shows will we have in the next twenty-five years?

As of January 2012, the five highest-rated primetime sitcoms are *The Big Bang Theory, Modern Family, 2 Broke Girls, Two and a Half Men* and *How I Met Your Mother.*[14] These TV shows are predominantly about good-looking single men who are highly accomplished in their professions and pretty single women who are unemployed or struggling financially. For example, the female characters on *Modern Family* are all stay-at-home moms. On *How I Met Your Mother,* Robin is a struggling journalist while Lily is a nursery school teacher. On *2 Broke Girls*, both leading ladies are model-pretty women who work as waitresses and can barely pay their rent. In *Two and Half Men*, all the female characters are stalkers, cleaning ladies, vindictive ex-wives or manipulative mothers. On *The Big Bang Theory*, Penny is the beautiful waitress whom all the male characters lust for. In amazing contrast, virtually all the male characters on these shows are wildly successful. On *How I Met Your Mother*, Ted is the youngest architect to ever build a New York skyscraper, Barney is a powerful executive who is always wearing a suit and Marshall is a corporate lawyer. On *Modern Family*, Mitchell is a lawyer, Jay owns a construction company and Phil is a real estate broker. On *Two and a Half Men*, Alan is a chiropractor, Charlie was a highly successful jingle writer and their newest edition, Walden, is a self-made billionaire. On

The Big Bang Theory, all the male characters are brilliant physicists and engineers. While this is a sexist portrayal of women and an inaccurate view of men, it showcases what many women seem to relate to and what many men seem to dream about. Today's most popular shows are predominantly about a single person's pursuit of career and romance. Within most of this, the family unit is missing.

Why don't we relate anymore to a husband and wife raising children in a home together?

Perhaps it is because the divorce rates in our country have become so high that most people simply did not experience being raised by both a father and mother. In Chapter 1, I gave you the staggering statistics that 45 to 50% of all first marriages in the U.S. end in divorce, 60 to 67% of all second marriages in the U.S. end in divorce and 70 to 73% of all third marriages in the U.S. end in divorce. I also told you that in 1980, the percentage of all U.S. births to unmarried women was 18.4% while in 2007, it had climbed to almost 40%. What an unfathomable statistic: that childbirths to unmarried women would more than double over one generation! At that rate, by 2015, half of all babies will be born out of wedlock, making illegitimacy rather than divorce the main cause of fatherlessness. As Christians, it is vital that we change this trend!

While not every person is called to be married (1 Corinthians 7), every marriage is called to be godly! We must teach and *practice* these biblical concepts so that we, as Christians, can reverse our current societal trend.

> Husbands, love your wives, just as Christ loved the church and gave himself up for her to make her holy.
>
> —Ephesians 5:25–26a

> However, each one of you also must love his wife as he loves himself, and the wife must respect her husband.
>
> —Ephesians 5:33

"I hate divorce," says the LORD God.

—Malachi 2:16

When we choose to go against God's teachings and begin to make up our own rules about marriage and family, bad things happen. Please consider these heart-wrenching statistics:[15]

Incarceration Rates
Young men who grow up in homes without fathers are *twice as likely* to end up in jail as those who come from traditional two-parent homes.

Criminal Activity
The likelihood that a young male will engage in criminal activity *doubles* if he is raised without a father and *triples* if he lives in a neighborhood with a high concentration of single-parent families.

Delinquency
77% of juvenile delinquents have parents who either divorced, separated or never married. By contrast, only 13% of juvenile delinquents come from families in which the biological father and mother are married to each other.

Achievement
Children from low-income, two-parent families outperform students from high-income, single-parent homes. Almost twice as

many high achievers come from two-parent homes as one-parent homes.

Confused Identities
Boys who grow up in father-absent homes are more likely than those in father-present homes to have trouble establishing appropriate sex roles and gender identity.

Behavioral Disorders
85% of all children who exhibit behavioral disorders come from fatherless homes.

Suicide
63% of youth suicides are from fatherless homes.

High School Dropouts
71% of all high school dropouts come from fatherless homes.

Brothers and sisters, the family unit is disintegrating. Our society, as a whole, no longer values having a man and woman get married, remain married and raise children together. While appreciated in concept, it is not seen very often in reality. Marriage is viewed by many today as an optional contract, one that can be broken if you "grow apart" or "fall out of love" or have "irreconcilable differences." Did you know that Mexico City lawmakers have recently proposed a two-year contract on marriage licenses? It's true. Just Google the words "Mexican 2 year marriage contract" and read all about it. Basically, because so many people are going through messy divorces and backing up their court systems, Mexican lawmakers are proposing a short-term marriage contract so that people can get out easier. Leonel Luna, the Mexico City assemblyman who coauthored the bill, said, "The proposal is, when the two-year period is up, if the relationship is not stable or harmonious, the contract simply ends. You wouldn't have to go through the tortuous process of divorce."[16] How crazy is that? Since when did a marriage become like a cell phone contract? Could you imagine hearing these wedding vows: "...to have and to hold, in sickness and in health, in good times and in bad, until 2014 when you part"? This idea may not be in the U.S. yet, but it certainly could come here. If our society continues to disregard God's word about marriage and family, this two-year optional marriage may be a real choice for you or your children one day.

As disciples of Jesus Christ, it is imperative that we teach God's word! Not only that, but our lives must also reflect Jesus to a dark world that desperately needs to see him! We must never back down from our God-given convictions about marriage and family. The epidemic of divorce and fatherlessness in the United States has serious consequences for children and is the cause of many of the social ills that people face today. According to 72.2% of the U.S. population, *fatherlessness is the most significant family or social problem facing America.*[17] David Blankenhorn, founder and president of the Institute for American Values, says, "The most urgent domestic challenge facing the United States...is the re-creation of fatherhood as a vital social role for men." Who is going to change this? The Christians!

I grew up in a single-parent home, as my mom and dad divorced when I was two years old. When I started dating Kim at age sixteen, I had no idea how to work out relationship problems. Praise God that her parents had been married for thirty-five years, so Kim was able to help teach me through what she had witnessed in her parents.

Later, as we were getting married at age twenty-two, I told Kim that I had no desire to ever be a father. I thought children just got in the way of career success and overall happiness. However, when I became a Christian at age twenty-three and saw loving fathers and respectful kids in the church, my heart changed. I became drawn to fatherhood. My point is that, before someone can change their heart, they have to see it in someone else. Most people will never understand the power of a strong marriage or the joy of fatherhood until they witness it in a friend. As Jesus said in Matthew 5:14, "You are the light of the world. A city on a hill cannot be hidden." Be the city on a hill! Be the light that this world needs to see! Christians hold the key to reversing this epidemic and reestablishing the importance of the family unit.

Overcoming Obesity by Living a Healthy Lifestyle and Balancing Social Media

Did you know that our nation is getting fatter? It's true! In 1995, no U.S. state had had an obesity rate above 20%. Today, *every U.S. state* has an obesity rate above 20%, except for one. The one state that has an obesity rate below 20% is Colorado, with 19.8% of their adults considered obese. However, at 19.8%, Colorado would have had the highest rate back in 1995.[18] This is a remarkable change over the last seventeen years and is a gigantic problem in our country today.

Obesity is defined as any person having a body mass index (BMI) of 30 or more. The BMI is a measurement based on a calculation using a person's weight and height. For example, a person who is 5 feet 5 inches and weighs 150 pounds would have a BMI of 25. However, if that same person weighed 180 pounds, the BMI would be 30. Although body mass index isn't always the best indicator for someone who has a lot of muscle, it is considered the best way to measure the general population.

A study, based on data collected in 2010, shows that a dozen states top 30% obesity, most of them in the South.[19] Mississippi topped the list for the seventh year in a row (not a good record to hold), followed by Alabama, West Virginia, Tennessee and Louisiana close behind. In 2006, only five years ago, Mississippi was the only state above 30%. Amazingly, no U.S. state decreased its level of obesity from the previous year. Do you hear what I am saying? We are getting fatter as a nation!

What does the Bible have to say about this?

Their destiny is destruction, their god is their stomach, and their glory is in their shame. Their mind is on earthly things.

—Philippians 3:19

Do not join those who drink too much wine
    or gorge themselves on meat,
for drunkards and gluttons become poor,
    and drowsiness clothes them in rags.

—Proverbs 23:20

For physical training is of some value, but godliness has value for all things.

—1 Timothy 4:8

Before we can help change the world, we must each examine ourselves. As Christians, we need to be fit simply because we are a reflection of Jesus to the world (2 Corinthians 3:18). We don't work out or eat right so that we can "fit in" or look a certain way. Of course not; it is all for the glory of God. As 1 Corinthians 3:9 and 16 tell us, we (the church) are God's building, God's temple. I wonder if the obesity rate within God's church is any different from that of the general public. I am not trying to make you feel uncomfortable; I am just trying to be real. If the preacher never talks about it and the Christians don't bring it up in Bible studies, then how would the obesity rate in the church be any different from that of the world? It may be a giant elephant in the room (no pun intended) and nobody wants to talk about it. Certainly there are Christians who have medical conditions that greatly affect their weight gain or limit their ability to exercise. We should be completely understanding of people in those situations. However, there are a lot Christians who are overweight simply because of their poor diet and/or lack of exercise. If we are going to *change the world* in this area, we must first *change the church*.

As a Christian, do you live a generally healthy lifestyle? Do you buy vegetables, fruits, pastas and meats from the grocery store and cook them in your home? Or do you simply have a supreme pizza delivered to your door and justify that you are now "eating your veggies"? If I came to your home and looked in your refrigerator (something I do whenever I am at a college student's apartment, by the way), what would I see? I know many college students and young professionals who eat out every day, often more than once per day. For some students, fast food is their main diet. That's crazy! While eating out at restaurants is fine in moderation, it should never be the main source of your meals. Sadly, this kind of diet usually stems from laziness and procrastination.

As a Christian, do you exercise regularly? Do you have a partner with whom you go to the gym or jog around campus? If not, I want to strongly encourage you to ask a friend to exercise with you regularly and/or hold you accountable.

Personally, I have been pretty strong about working out throughout my life but not so strong about eating right. It is enjoyable for me to go work out or play basketball, but it is also enjoyable for me to eat a hamburger, fries and a milkshake. This is not good. Two months ago, Kim and I studied the Daniel 1 with our kids and decided to follow the "Daniel diet" for one week. For us, it meant just eating fruits, vegetables, whole grains and fish... this included eating no beef or chicken. This diet changed the way I think. After one week, I felt great and I realized that I did not miss eating meat (slow down—I still eat beef and chicken today, but only on occasion—I call myself "a schizophrenic pescatarian"). I have become very convicted about my need to exercise regularly *and* eat right. Six weeks ago, Kim and I committed to doing the P90X workouts every morning together and eating really healthy. Even though I have wanted to quit on occasion, having a partner doing it with me has made all the difference. When I made this decision to change six weeks ago, I was 6'1" and weighed 210 pounds. Today, I weigh 193 pounds. I am very excited about this. Even though Jesus was Lord of my life, I feel that I have not allowed him to be Lord of my eating for a really long time. As a Christian, there can never be an area of your life where you do not allow Jesus to reign. I thank God that he allows us to repent. Do you need to change your diet or exercise habits?

With today's young people, I have noticed an ugly trend: Hard work is out and laziness is in. Obviously, this is a general statement and not everyone from the age of eighteen to thirty fits into this category. However, I believe that too many young people don't want to work hard for their degree or for their income. They would rather it be given to them. Too many college students and young professionals feel that they are entitled to certain benefits in life and don't want to have to work hard to achieve things. There is even a huge trend currently in high school and college to wear pajamas to school. Even stores like Abercrombie & Fitch and Aéropostale are responding to the trend by creating new pajama lines.[20] While I am sure some students wear pajamas to school because it is fashionable and trendy, I believe others do it because it communicates a message: "I'm lazy and I'd rather be back in bed."

I was on the University of Florida campus last month when I saw a college student wearing a Nike T-shirt that said, "LAZY BUT TALENTED" in large block lettering. It had the big Nike swoosh right under the words. The fact that Nike would make a shirt promoting this idea shows how popular a concept this has become among young people. When I saw the shirt, I thought to myself, "I wonder how this shirt would have gone over in the previous generation? Would people from the 1970s or 1980s embrace this concept?" Last week, I saw another college student wearing a T-shirt that read: "Hard work never hurt anybody, but why take the chance?" Obviously, companies are making these shirts because young people embrace this way of thinking. Does this concept offend you as a young person? Why do you think it is considered "cool" to wear a shirt like this, promoting the idea that you are lazy or don't like to work hard? Remember that Proverbs 10:4 says, "Lazy hands make a man poor, but diligent hands bring wealth." In my opinion, the concept that it is cool to be lazy has become a theme for many young people. This way of thinking has an effect on our epidemic of obesity.

Let's talk about social media for a minute and how this affects our obesity problem. Did you know that the average young American spends practically every waking minute—except for the time in school—using a smart phone, computer, television or other electronic device?[20] According to the New York Times, those ages eight to eighteen spend more than 7.5 hours *per day* with such devices, and that does not count the 1.5 hours per day that youths spend texting or the 0.5 hours per day talking on the phone. According to U.S. News, college students spend an average of almost five hours per day watching TV or playing video games, and that does not include texting or talking on the phone. Many studies have linked screen time with attention problems, as "ADHD [attention-deficit hyperactivity disorder] is ten times more common today than it was twenty years ago," says Dr. Dimitri Christakis, the George Adkins Professor of Pediatrics at the University of Washington.[21] Some studies have even shown that the more screen time a person uses, the greater risk they have of obesity.[22] How is your use of "screen time"? How many hours per day do you spend on the computer, on the television, talking on the phone or texting? Do you feel the need to constantly update your profile on Facebook or follow someone on Twitter? Would your day feel empty or boring if you did not have these devices to use? Could you fast from all technology for a few days or does the thought of that make you cringe? I want to encourage you to take a "world fast"—no computers, no radio or music of any kind, no television, no newspaper and no cell phone. Radical, huh? Are you up for it? Try a "world fast" for a few days and see what it tells you about your dependence on technology.

Let's face it: Many young people (and older people too) have become addicted to social media. They are constantly on Facebook or Twitter or are multitasking by surfing the Internet while watching television. In many cases, these addictions are causing people to be less interested in working out, jogging or going for a walk. For many people, social media is increasing their risk of becoming obese. While these incredible electronic devices and media outlets are not going to go away anytime soon, we as Christians must learn to control them rather than letting our lust for these devices control us.

In a world of imbalance, the disciples of Jesus must learn to find balance. We must be able to balance our needs for exercise and healthy eating with our desires for entertainment and media. I see too many college students and young professionals who continually give in to their lust for "screen time" while ignoring the other needs in their life. As more and more disciples get their priorities right, the Christian nation will be able to help lead our country to overcome obesity by living a healthy lifestyle.

Taking Care of the Poor and the Needy

According to the Bread of the Mighty Food Bank, the poverty level in the United States is 14.3% (in my county, Alachua County, it is 26.9%). The percentage of U.S. households with children who have a food hardship is 23.4%. That means one out of four children in the U.S. faces hunger regularly. As Christians, this has to bother us. God is very serious about his children taking care of the poor and needy around them. We need to care because God cares!

When our country first started, it was the churches that took care of the poor and the needy. The Christians made extra clothes, cooked extra food, and served it to the poor while looking them in the eye. Today, that job has largely been _outsourced to the government_. Today, the government taxes the working force so that they can distribute welfare checks and food stamps. This has caused the average American's heart to become hard toward serving the poor and disconnected from the real needs. It has even caused some of the poor to feel embittered or ungrateful for the help that they receive, feeling that the government is not doing enough to serve them. This, too, is our fault because we have made serving the poor impersonal. This was never God's plan. God's plan has always been for *his children* to serve the poor. When we stray from God's plan, we will always fail.

> He who gives to the poor will lack nothing,
> but he who closes his eyes to them receives many curses.
>
> —Proverbs 28:27

> Religion that God our Father accepts as pure and faultless is this: to look after orphans and widows in their distress and to keep oneself from being polluted by the world.
>
> —James 1:27

> He who oppresses the poor shows contempt for their Maker,
> but whoever is kind to the needy honors God.
>
> —Proverbs 14:31

> If a man shuts his ears to the cry of the poor,
> he too will cry out and not be answered.
>
> —Proverbs 21:13

> James, Peter and John, those reputed to be pillars, gave me and Barnabas the right hand of fellowship when they recognized the grace given to me. They agreed that we should go to the Gentiles, and they to the Jews. All they asked was that we should continue to remember the poor, the very thing I was eager to do.
>
> —Galatians 2:9–10

Galatians 2:9–10 gives us amazing insight into the heart of first-century Christians to take care of the poor. We have Peter,

James and John (the three apostles known for being the closest to Jesus) in a room talking with Paul (starter of twenty-one churches and leader of the first-century movement) and Barnabas. Talk about an all-star cast of Christians! As Paul and Barnabas are going on missionary journeys and are completely focused on spreading the gospel to outside cities, Peter, James and John remind them to serve the poor. Don't just preach the word, but also serve the poor. That's amazing! Paul and Barnabas respond by basically saying, "Absolutely. We definitely intend to do that."

One of the ways that we work together as Christians in Gainesville to serve the poor is with our biannual Canned Food Drive. It is led by Hank and Allison Middleton, two recent graduates from our campus ministry. Most canned food drives are done by placing a box in the church foyer for members to fill up with nonperishable foods. However, this will only allow your church members to give and will most likely have minimal impact. At GCC, we help and encourage the residents of Gainesville to give and we raise a lot more food because of it. We start by going to numerous local grocery stores and getting 1500 to 2000 paper bags. We then write up a letter explaining who we are and what we are doing, make a ton of copies, and staple one letter to the outside of each grocery bag. Then the fun begins. We get a group of thirty to seventy people to meet up on a Saturday morning, and we take a few hours to walk through specific neighborhoods and drop off one bag on each doorstep. In the letter attached to the grocery bag, we explain that we will return in one week to collect the bag full of nonperishable foods, if they choose to give. The following Saturday, we return to the same neighborhoods and collect all the food. We have a blast! In general, one out of every three houses will participate.

The first time we did this, we raised 2200 pounds of food (one pound of food is equivalent to one meal for the poor and homeless)! To put this in perspective, the largest one-time gift ever given to the Gainesville Bread of the Mighty Food Bank was about 2000 pounds. We broke the city record on our first try! Amazing! As we have gotten more organized over the past few years, we have been able to raise more food. In recent food drives, we have collected up to 3500 pounds of food. To God be the glory! The best part is when Hank and Allison drive all the food over to the food bank. They said it feels like being Santa Clause on Christmas morning. While some adults attend our GCC Canned Food Drives, I would guess that 90% of the people who participate are college students.

Some worldwide or citywide problems are too large for you to tackle by yourself. However, if you work together as a team, the Christian nation can make a huge impact.

Another way that we work together to serve the needy in Gainesville is by taking care of the elderly. About five years ago, our church began a relationship with the Emeritus Assisted Living Facility here in Gainesville. This facility is located about three miles from the University of Florida and is an assisted living and retirement community that offers varied levels of care. Some of the residents are in wheelchairs, while others suffer from Alzheimer's or dementia. As a church, we have adopted Emeritus into our family. Every Sunday, we hold a thirty- to forty-minute worship service in their facility, because most of the residents are unable to travel. We also hold a Tuesday afternoon Bible discussion group led by our deacon of Emeritus and my good friend, Frank Bogle (who is 78 years old). Additionally, we have a once per month "Cookies and Conversations" evening where we bring a lot of snacks and just sit down to talk with the residents. They love it! Many of them have no family and are so grateful that anyone, especially young people, would want to visit with them. While some of our college students and young professionals attend the Emeritus Sunday services, many of them attend the "Cookies and Conversations." It has been wonderful to serve the residents! God has blessed our efforts beyond what we thought were possible as we have seen five people baptized at Emeritus! One of them, Bowtie Jack, has already passed away and I had the privilege of speaking at his funeral. I wore one of his bowties that day, in honor of him.

A third way that we work together in Gainesville to serve the poor and the needy is through our Blood Drive. Led by Norman Classen, we get two large bloodmobiles from the Blood Bank to come to our church service every four months and we encourage all of our members to give. People sign up to give blood ranging from two hours before church begins to two hours after church is over. Last year, the Gainesville Christian Church gave 120 pints of blood, the largest amount given by any single group in the city by far. Once again, when the Christians work together, we can really serve the needy and give much glory to God!

Other projects we have done recently include a twenty-four-hour basketball fundraiser (most of the participants were high school students, college students or young professionals) for Arco Iris Hospital in La Paz, Bolivia. As a group, we raised over $5000 by renting a gym, playing hoops all day and night, and asking our families and friends to sponsor us. It was so cool (and very tiring!). We have also done a clothing drive in the past where we encouraged everyone to go through their closets and get every piece of clothing that they had not worn in the past six months and donate it to the poor. As a church, we gave away so much clothing, it was incredible. I am not trying to give you all the answers, because I do not have them. Rather, I am trying to stir your mind and get your creative juices flowing. What has God put on your heart to do for the poor?

There is so much poverty around us. I know many Christians who have a huge heart for the poor, bigger than mine. If that is you, then I want to thank you for your love and inspiration. We need more Christians, all Christians, to care about this. God has given us a task and we dare not let him down.

How Can We Change the World?

While there are some problems that we can handle individually, there are other issues that we must tackle as a group. Some of the biggest moral and spiritual problems of our world—sex before marriage, racism, fatherlessness and the lack of a family unit, obesity, and rampant poverty—could be solved (or at least seriously minimized) by Christians working together and praying together. I hope that you will catch God's dream and be a part of the solution.

(Small group discussion questions are on the following page.)

Small Group Discussion Questions for Chapter Eight

1. How have you seen sex before marriage be harmful to young people? Have you decided to be abstinent before marriage? Why or why not? Are you willing to talk to your friends and peers about abstinence?

2. How have you seen racism and discrimination in our country? Do you agree that "Sunday is the most segregated day of the week"? Do you believe that young people can help solve this problem? Do you have friends from different nationalities or do most of your friends look like you?

3. Why do you think primetime television has switched its focus from family life to single life over the last generation? What is your relationship like with your father and how has it influenced your life? How can young people today reestablish the importance of the family unit in our country?

4. Do you think obesity is a problem in our society today? Do you live a healthy lifestyle of diet and exercise or do you need to make some changes? Is it "cool" today to appear lazy or unmotivated? How has social media affected students and young professionals, and are we addicted to it?

5. Do you feel that most people in our country (or even in the church) are focused on helping the poor? Why or why not? What are some successful projects that you have been a part of in the past to help the poor? What are some new projects that God has put on your heart that you would like to see your church/ministry/group of friends take on? What will it take to accomplish this?

Chapter Nine

The Time Is Now!

Maximus: "Brothers, what we do in life echoes in eternity."

—*Gladiator*

What we do today will affect tomorrow. The decisions you make right now will help to change the spiritual destinies of many other men and women. The way you choose to live will echo in eternity! However, you must understand that the time to act in now!

> He [Felix the governor] sent for Paul and listened to him as he spoke about faith in Christ Jesus. As Paul discoursed on righteousness, self-control and the judgment to come, Felix was afraid and said, "That's enough for now! You may leave. *When I find it convenient,* I will send for you."
> —Acts 24:24b–25, emphasis added

There will never be a convenient time to change the world! Often times when there are big tasks that need to be accomplished in our lives, we are tempted to say to ourselves, "I'll do it later." Whether we are talking about starting a diet, mowing the yard, studying for an exam or getting closer to God, many people view the future as a better launching date than the present. I have heard many college students say, "When I graduate from college, then I'll get serious about my relationship with God." However, when they graduate from college, they get caught up in their full-time job and begin to rationalize their procrastination. They begin to think, "Later on in life, maybe when I get married, then I'll settle down and focus on God." However, once they get married they will be tempted to think, "When we start having kids I'll get serious about God, because I want my children to be raised in a church." The cycle goes on and on. The problem with procrastination is that it has no end.

The time is now! Our country's morals and overall spirituality have been on a major decline from the last generation until now. You can see this decline by examining the changes in popular television shows, but you can also see it in the U.S. statistics about teenage suicide, obesity, fatherlessness, abortions, sex before marriage, child births out of wedlock, racism and pornography usage. Our country needs leadership! Our country needs God! Our country needs the *young people today to stand up for God* and say, "Enough is enough! I am willing to do my part to help change the world!"

A Golden Opportunity

As a college student, do you realize the opportunity for *maximum impact* that is in front of you? On every college and university campus around the US, thousands of students live and study on basically one square mile of real estate. At the University of Florida, we have approximately 50,000 students, most of them either living on campus or in the surrounding apartment complexes. That's amazing! That means you either live beside or cross paths with hundreds of people in your peer group every day. This is such a rare opportunity. Once you leave campus life, this opportunity will most likely never present itself to you again. Do you realize that? As a forty-year-old married man with two children, I have a difficult time meeting other people who are in my place in life. I reach out to all kinds of people, but rarely find someone who is like me. In college, most everyone you meet will be in your stage of life.

Additionally, people in college are usually very open to friendships and are not held back by economic status. After all, students are generally in the same place financially: poor. Think about it: Does it matter if you are majoring in English education and you meet someone in college who is majoring in premed? Does that difference hinder your friendship? Not at all. However, let's fast forward thirty years. As a fifty-year-old, imagine that you have been teaching high school English for the last three decades while the other person has been performing brain surgeries. If you meet at age fifty, how would that meeting go? I can tell you from firsthand experience that it is much more difficult to befriend and/ or convert someone at that stage in life. Think about the people you know of who are highly successful in business, politics, movies and medicine. Could you reach Reece Witherspoon or Barack Obama or Oprah today? Probably not. However, if you were in college with them back in the day, could you have reached them at that point? Of course. You see, once people become highly successful or affluent, their circle of trusted friends becomes much smaller. They usually wonder why you are trying to befriend them and what you might want from them. This is hardly ever the case in college.

Love God, Change the World

If you are going to help change this world, the time for action is now! Don't wait until your class load lightens up, your job gets easier or your minister "gets it." I have three questions for you:

1. If not you, then who?
2. If not now, then when?
3. If not here, then where?

In Chapter 1 of this book, I asked you a question: Do you hear the alarm that God is sounding? I gave you these passages from the book of Joel (all emphasis added):

> Hear this, you elders;
>> *listen, all who live in the land.*
> Has anything like this ever happened in your days
>> or in the days of your forefathers? (1:2)

> A nation has invaded my land,
>> powerful and without number;
> it has the teeth of a lion,
>> the fangs of a lioness. (1:6)

> *Put on sackcloth, O priests, and mourn;*
>> wail, you who minister before the altar. (1:13a)

> *Declare a holy fast;*
>> call a sacred assembly. (1:14a)

> Blow the trumpet in Zion;
>> *sound the alarm* on my holy hill. (2:1)

> *"Even now,"* declares the LORD,
>> *"return to me with all your heart."* (2:12a)

> Return to the LORD your God,
>> for he is gracious and compassionate. (2:13)

> Gather the people,
>> *consecrate the assembly;*
> *bring together the elders,*
>> *gather the children,*
>> *those nursing at the breast.*
> *Let the bridegroom leave his room*
>> *and the bride her chamber.* (2:16)

> Proclaim this among the nations:
>> *Prepare for war!*
> *Rouse the warriors!* (3:9a)

This paragraph from Chapter 1 is also worth repeating: Do you notice the severity of the alarm? Everybody was expected to respond to it, including the infants who were being nursed by their mothers. You were expected to respond even if it was your wedding today and you were just moments from the ceremony. Wow! The call was radical:

DROP EVERYTHING YOU ARE DOING
AND COME TOGETHER TO CHANGE THE WORLD!

It did not matter who you were or what you were doing. This was a call for all of God's people to come together, hear the alarm, notice the devastation, and repent of *their sins*. They had become a nation of self-indulgent people who had begun to value material things over spiritual things. God was not willing to change the devastation until his people were ready to change.

Brothers and sisters, I believe that God's calling is for *us to repent* so that *we can change the world!* It is time to rouse the warriors! There is much to do and we cannot do it alone. As Jesus said in Mark 10:27, "With man this is impossible, but not with God; all things are possible with God." I firmly believe that the high school students, the college students and the young professionals *hold the key* to changing the course of the world. Are you up for it? Are you willing to do your part as an individual? Are you willing to work with a group of Christians to do your part collectively? I hope so.

My message is simple: Let's love God and change the world!

My Personal Testimony

I was born on October 26, 1971 in Gainesville, Florida, a city mostly known for having the University of Florida. Gainesville is an amazing city with a population of about 100,000 people, with approximately 60,000 of those being college students. When I was fifteen years old, I began attending a large denominational church, which preached from the Bible and taught me to have a basic faith in God. However, I can honestly say that, at that time, I did not make Jesus the Lord of my life. Instead of becoming a Christian, I merely became religious. Even though I attended church frequently, my life throughout high school looked like everybody else's life—going out to nightclubs, getting drunk, cursing, and engaging in sexual immorality with my girlfriend. I would go out to parties on Saturday night and sing the church songs on Sunday morning. I was quite the hypocrite. I remember that at the end of most Sunday sermons the preacher would ask the audience, "Who in here needs to accept Christ today?" While I would never raise my hand for fear of being embarrassed, I would still pray the prayer in my heart as the preacher led the prayer aloud. I must have prayed that prayer dozens of times, just in case it did not work previously. Can you relate to this?

When I went to college at the University of North Florida in Jacksonville, I pretty much stopped attending church all together. I had become tired of the hypocrisy that I saw in my own life and in my peer group who attended church with me. I joined a fraternity, got involved in student government and had a steady girlfriend. I was still fairly religious and full of good morals as I never smoked, rarely got drunk and tried to make a difference on campus. I eventually became president of my fraternity and ran for student body vice president (I came in second). I was turning into a good person, but still not living as a Christian. Can you relate to this?

After I graduated college with my bachelor's degree in mathematics, I married my high school sweetheart, Kim, and soon joined the U.S. Navy as a Nuclear Reactor Operator designated for submarines. Even though I had my college degree, I decided to enlist in the Navy because the nuclear field was the only job I was interested in and joining as a nuclear officer right out of college was not available to me. However, I was told that if I succeeded in the enlisted nuclear power program, I would be selected for Officer Candidate School (OCS) very quickly and then be sent to the officer nuclear power school. Thus, I was highly motivated to succeed and completely naive as to how difficult this would be for me to be one of the few enlisted men with a college degree. To make matters worse, when I arrived in Orlando in May 1995, I found out that the enlisted nuclear power school building was located right next to the officer nuclear power school building. They faced each other. Every day when I walked into my building, I was reminded that men who used to be my peers or whom I used to lead in college were now my superiors and I had to salute them. It was very humbling for me. I did not understand it at the time, but God was molding my character and humbling my heart so that one day I would be open to his word.

One moment I will never forget was the day we were having one of our regular "work parties." A work party would happen about once per month where the enlisted men would clean every inch of the submarine. It would usually take all day. I was on my hands and knees scrubbing a piece of equipment near the bulkhead (a wall) when an officer who was perhaps two or three years older than I walked by and pointed at the ground saying, "You missed a spot." As he walked away, my eyes began to tear up. I felt so belittled. "What am I doing here?" I thought to myself. I got angry at God and thought, "God, why did you lead me here? Why is my application for OCS taking so long to be processed? I don't want to be here any longer!" Literally, if I could have run away, I would have.

By the grace of God, I was able to graduate number one in my class from Nuclear Field "A" school and then graduate in the top five percent of my class from Nuclear Power school. Soon after, I received word that I had been selected to attend OCS in Pensacola, Florida. Needless to say, I was overjoyed! After eighteen months, I was finally going to be an officer! All of that hard work—putting in seventy hours per week at school, unable to bring any material home due to its confidential nature, being away from my wife from 5:00 a.m. to 9:00 p.m. on most days—finally paid off! I was sent to Charleston, South Carolina to finish the enlisted nuclear power school and then would be transferred to OCS in Pensacola.

Once in Charleston, Kim and I began looking for a church to attend. As a young married couple of two years, we felt that it was right to worship God with a church family and that I would now have the time to do it. We attended four different churches on four consecutive Sundays, each time leaving with the feeling that we had not found the right one—one was very quiet, one had everyone speaking in tongues at the same time, one was all white people...

we were getting discouraged. There were certain qualities that we knew were right in a church and we just were not finding them. We decided to have church in our house the next Sunday and the two of us sang the only song that we could remember: "Amazing Grace." We sang it three times during our house church. I read from the book of Daniel as Kim sat on our bed and listened. Looking back on it, the authenticity of our worship made it one of the best church services I have ever attended.

About two days after our private house church service, a college student at Kim's job stood up at a work meeting and asked if anyone would be interested in donating money to a downtown cleanup effort his church was doing to raise funds for foreign missions. Kim came home so excited and wanted to see if I was willing to contribute. Even though we had not been attending church much during our first two years of marriage, we knew that the Bible called us to give a portion of our income to God. Thus, we had been setting aside 10% of our income into a savings account and we had promised each other that we would give this to a church when we found a good one. After about two years of doing this, our account had built up a little bit. Consequently, we gave the college student $300 from our savings account and he ended up inviting us to church. We decided to attend the next Sunday and we were blown away at what we found. It was a racially mixed group of Christians where the minister preached strongly from the word of God and the people strove to live it out! We loved it! We began attending regularly, although we knew that we were leaving for Florida in one month so that I could attend Officer Candidate School. Thus, we turned down people's requests to study the Bible with us.

About two weeks before my departure for Pensacola, I was playing basketball on the Navy base when I got tripped up during the game and broke my right arm. The injury was so severe that I needed emergency surgery the next day in order to tease the fibers of my bone back in place. It was at this time that I was informed by the doctor that I would have to miss my appointment to OCS due to the injury and would need to stay in Charleston, South Carolina for the next three to four months to recover. On top of that, I would have to reapply for OCS and may not be selected again due to the existence of a permanent screw in my newly repaired right arm. I was crushed (to say the least). All of my dreams were crashing down around me. I now questioned God in a way that I never had before. All I could think about was, "Why? If you love me as much as your Bible says, then why would you let this happen to me?" Sometimes, we can only see one piece while God sees the entire puzzle.

For the next three weeks, I was given convalescent leave from my naval duties so that I could be at my home on base and recover. Amazingly, the disciples from the church began to come over and bring us food—really good, homemade dinners! We were super grateful. After about one week of recovery time, our friends Monty and Sandy Drenner as well as Doyle and Mia Chisholm asked us if they could study the Bible with us. We were just sitting at home, so we agreed.

I still remember the first question that Monty asked me: "Troy, how well do you know the Bible?" Everything in me wanted to give a prideful response to that question: "I've been around the Bible for years" or "I've heard many sermons before." However, I knew that if he just said, "Turn to the book of Ephesians" or "Open up to 2 Timothy," I would have to turn to my table of contents to find it. Therefore, I just answered him, "I don't know it as well as I should." We then began an amazing series of Bible studies on God's word, the Lordship of Jesus, sin and repentance, baptism, the cross and the church. As they encouraged us to make a commitment to read the word daily, I felt so challenged to become someone whom I had never become before. I was so excited and yet somewhat afraid. After the study on the Lordship of Jesus, I realized that I had never really committed to becoming a disciple of Jesus. I had become religious, even spiritual—but not a follower of Jesus. Even though I had considered myself a Christian for many years, the Scriptures showed me that I had not made Jesus my Lord. Kim and I went home that night and cried together in our living room. I told my wife, "There's a part of me that wishes that I had never met these people, because now I have to change my life." I felt like Neo in the movie *The Matrix* when he contemplated taking the blue pill so that he could go back to his old ways and forget about what he had just been taught. However, I knew that was the cowardly choice and ultimately the wrong decision. So after praying together, Kim and I confessed our sins to each other (sins that we had never told each other before), and vowed to one another and God that we would help each other to live as disciples of Jesus. On July 14, 1996, we were baptized into Christ and born again (Acts 2:38, John 3:3–5). It was glorious! It was the beginning of our new life in Christ!

Now that I have been a true Christian for sixteen years, one of my deepest convictions is this: If God can reach me, he can reach anybody! I was simply a religious kid who grew up in a small city. I constantly "rode the fence" between God and the world and had very little ambition to advance God's kingdom. In all honesty, I was more interested in building my own kingdom and yet still having God as a slice of my life. When I made the declaration that "Jesus is Lord" and got baptized, God transformed me into a radical disciple and exchanged my worldly dreams for his dreams. After my baptism, I soon received a medical discharge from the Navy, and I went into the full-time ministry in August 1997.

As I write this book in 2012, I have now been a disciple of Jesus for the past sixteen years. I have had the privilege of returning to my hometown of Gainesville, Florida in August 1999 to start a church with a mission team of thirty-five other disciples. To God's glory, the Gainesville Christian Church has grown today to 295 disciples with about 350 people in attendance every Sunday. I have also had the joy of helping to raise up and train dozens of men and women campus ministers and send them out to lead other ministries throughout the U.S. and South America. Additionally, I have been able to work with a dozen campus ministers from around the world on a Campus Service Team to help mobilize college students and college graduates to have tremendous domestic and international impact. This Campus Service Team has also been able to help organize International Campus Ministry Conferences around the world. In 2010, we had twenty-two different conferences globally, including bringing 2200 U.S. college students to Chicago for the U.S. ICMC.

I am so grateful to God for how he has changed my marriage and the direction of my life. He has given me spiritual dreams and godly ambitions that I never had before. The driving desire of my life today is to love God and change the world. I hope that you will join me.

—Troy A. Criss

End Notes

1. www.divorcestatistics.org, info according to Jennifer Baker, Forest Institute of Professional Psychology, Springfield.

2. Stephanie J. Ventura, "Changing Patterns of Nonmarital Childbearing in the United States," National Center for Health Statistics, May 2009.

3. Jennifer Marshall, "Sanctioning Illegitimacy: Our National Character Is at Stake," Family Research Council, 3/28/97.

4. www.abort73.com/abortion_facts/us_abortion_facts.

5. www.xxxchurch.com/whyporn/.

6. www.internet-filter-review.toptenreviews.com, article by Jerry Ropelato.

7. www.aacap.org/cs/root/facts_for_families.

8. Mike Taliaferro, *The Lion Never Sleeps* (Woburn, MA: Discipleship Publications International 2003).

9. www.wikipedia.org/wiki/Usain_bolt.

10. Rocky quotes: www.imdb.com/title/tt0084602/quotes.

11. The Gospel Advocate Commentary.

12. www.acgreen.com/abstinence/statistics.html.

13. Gainesville Sun newspaper article from Feb 8, 2012, written by the Associated Press.

14. www.csmonitor.com/commentary/opinion.

15. www.fatherhood.about.com.

16. http://www.reuters.com/article/2011/09/29/us-mexico-marriage-idUSTRE78S6TX20110929.

17. www.fathers.com article: "The Extent of Fatherlessness".

18. Gainesville Sun newspaper article, written by the Associated Press.

19. Ibid.

20. www.sfgate.com/sfmoms/2012/01/19 article: "Should teens be allowed to wear pajamas to school?".

21. www.nytimes.com/2010 article: "If your kids are awake, they're probably online".

22. www.usnews.com article: "Too much screen time can threaten attention span".

Illumination Publishers International

For the best in Christian writing and audio instruction, go to the Illumination Publishers website. We're committed to producing in-depth teaching that will inform, inspire and encourage Christians to a deeper and more committed walk with God. You can email us at our website below.

www.ipibooks.com